GERMAN

This book is intended for all who wish to learn to read,
write and speak German, and has been specially designed to
enable the student to develop his powers as quickly and as
easily as possible in all three. The section on pronunciation
is very comprehensive and by following it carefully the
reader should have no difficulty in acquiring a fair, if not
good, German accent. Each chapter ends with exercises to
test the student's progress, a key to which is given at the
end of the book.

TEACH YOURSELF BOOKS

GERMAN

A book of self-instruction in German,
based on the work by Sir John Adams,
M.A., LL.D., completely revised and
enlarged by Sydney W. Wells, B.A., and
further revised by E. S. Jenkins, B.A.

TEACH YOURSELF BOOKS
Hodder and Stoughton

First printed in this form 1938
Reset and revised edition 1971
Sixth impression 1977

This volume is published in the U.S.A. by David McKay Company Inc., 750 Third Avenue, New York, N.Y. 10017

ISBN 0 340 05788 2

Printed in Great Britain
for Hodder and Stoughton Paperbacks, a division of
Hodder and Stoughton Ltd., Mill Road, Dunton Green,
Sevenoaks, Kent (Editorial Office; 47 Bedford Square,
London WC1 3DP)
by Richard Clay (The Chaucer Press), Ltd., Bungay, Suffolk

PREFACE

WE have travelled a long way on the road since the English-man, tall and skinny, with sandy hair and protruding teeth, was made the butt of ridicule on the Continental stage, and his attempts to speak a foreign tongue were found either irritating or excruciatingly funny.

We have progressed much, too, in our approach to the study of foreign languages. We are not so content to signal and gesticulate for our food in a foreign restaurant, and our eyes no longer flash with indignation at these "damned foreigners" who cannot speak the King's English. It used to be quite common, too, for a well-educated man to turn out a creditable essay in French or German on the fossil iguanodon, yet be distressingly inarticulate when called upon to order a second-class railway ticket or a dinner. Amusing mistakes, of course, will always be made. There is the Scot, for instance, who translated "J'aime la langue française" by: "I love the tall French girl", or the German who said in great indignation to the waiter in a London restaurant: "I am here since ten minutes—when do I become a sausage!" He had forgotten that bekommen in English is *to get*, while the English *become* is in German werden.

Most of the difficulties of years ago were due to an undue importance given to grammar and Classical subject-matter: the teaching did not help the practical man who wanted to travel. It is claimed for this book that the interests of such people are studied throughout. The classified vocabularies should prove very helpful, and it is hoped that the student will find that the bug-bear of German declensions loses some of its terrors as presented here.

Anyone who follows this course conscientiously should be able to read, write and speak the German language with some measure of success. His accuracy and his fluency will depend not only on his native ability but also on his determination to keep at it regularly: a short time every day over a long period is much better than gigantic efforts every now and then.

SYDNEY W. WELLS.

INTRODUCTION

To know a language properly implies the power of using it freely for three different purposes: reading, writing and speaking.

Those who learn a foreign language may desire to learn it for all three purposes, or for one or two of them only. This work has been designed to enable the student to develop his powers as quickly and as easily as possible in all three. A language is a vast field, which can never be fully explored, and learning a language means hard work, careful thought and constant practice. If the student thinks he is going to speak or write or read German in a few months by means of a lesson or two done now and then, he had better give up the idea completely, for he is wasting his time. But this work, if followed conscientiously, will enable the average student not only to read German, but also to write and speak it in a fairly simple way.

The student without exceptional facilities must get into the habit of reading aloud, asking himself questions aloud and answering them himself—always, or as often as possible, aloud. The learning of words is important. To a large extent the vocabulary has been carefully kept up-to-date and thoroughly modern, with an eye to those who wish to read modern literature, to listen in to German broadcasts, or to travel on the Continent. These words should be mastered *somehow*, even if it means learning them off in lists. You must always have the subject in your mind. When you cast your eye on a thing, if you have known the German for it and forgotten, do not fail to look it up again at the *first* opportunity.

Conversational power is what you make it yourself. Not much has been given in actual conversations in this book, but all the exercises given are conversational in tone and subject matter. Make up your own conversations by rearranging the sentences given here.

A Key to the Exercises is given. This should be used sensibly. Do your exercise *before* consulting the Key, and then correct your own. Afterwards, do the exercises the other way round, testing your translation of the Key with the original exercises.

The student should revise constantly. In the scope of this little work it is impossible to give a thorough revision, but the student should, after every three lessons, go back and quickly refresh his mind on grammar and vocabulary.

As all the Exercises have their counterpart in the Key, no Vocabulary is given. But as many as possible of the words as they occur should be thoroughly committed to memory in order to render easier the task of translating subsequent exercises.

The section on Pronunciation is full and if the student follows it carefully he should have no difficulty in acquiring a fair pronunciation, if not a good one. If he can get native help, so much the better.

One word of warning: we have kept all the exercises in this book within certain limits. We have attempted nothing very clever, nothing "high-falutin'", and you must also school yourselves to this. As soon as you start trying difficult constructions you will find yourselves in deep water. Keep your sentences fairly short and make sure of the matter given you here before attempting anything else.

If you would like to add a little reading of continuous German prose you could not do better than buy Guerber's *Märchen und Erzählungen*, Part I (Harrap), after the fourth or fifth lesson of this work. These Märchen, or tales, may strike you as childish, but if you can overcome this, you will find that the easy style and constant repetition will give you a confidence which is very important.

CONTENTS

ix

PART I

§ I. THE GERMAN ALPHABET

Some German books are still to be found with Gothic letters, although modern books and newspapers are printed in Roman type, and German typewriters are fitted with Roman letters. It would be useful, therefore, for the student to familiarize himself with the German alphabet (see pages 12 and 13) after he has worked through this book.

Note 1.—There are five vowels: a, e, i, o, u, and there are the further combinations ai (ai), au (au), ei (ai), eu (ɔi), ie (i).

Of the above, a, o, u and au may *modify*, *i.e.* change their sound. They are then written and pronounced: ä (ɛ), ö (ø or œ), ü (y), äu (ɔi). The two dots are referred to as the Umlaut, meaning a change of sound.

Note 2.—There are several *digraphs* or *trigraphs*, *i.e.* groups of two or three consonants with a single sound:

ch	pronounced	ç or x	ss	pronounced	s
ck	,,	k	sch	,,	ʃ
ph	,,	f	th	,,	t

N.B.—Note 3 and pages 12 and 13 refer to the Gothic letters only and should be left until the student has worked through the book. He should, however, look at page 14, as one letter from the Gothic alphabet has been retained in modern German, before passing on to the section on German pronunciation.

Note 3.—The small round ſ is used only at the end of a word, even if this word is the first part of a compound word:

> Glas (glass)
> bis (until) and bisher (until now)
> Staatsmann (statesman)

English	German Characters		Pronuncia-tion[1]
	Printed	Written	
A a (ä)	𝔄 a (ä)		ʼɑː (ʼɛ)
B b	𝔅 b		beː
C c	ℭ c		tseː
D d	𝔇 d		deː
E e	𝔈 e		ʼeː
F f	𝔉 f		ʼɛf
G g	𝔊 g		geː
H h	ℌ h		hɑː
I i	ℑ i		ʼiː
J j	ℑ j		jɔt
K k	𝔎 k		kɑː
L l	𝔏 l		ʼɛl
M m	𝔐 m		ʼɛm

[1] For the Pronunciation, see § 2, Preliminary Note.

| English | German Characters | | Pronuncia-tion |
	Printed	Written	
N n	ℜ n		'ɛn
O o (ö)	𝔒 o (ö)		'oː ('ø)
P p	𝔓 p		peː
Q q	𝔔 q		kuː
R r	ℜ r		'ɛr
S s	𝔖 ſ ß s		'ɛs
T t	𝔗 t		teː
U u (ü)	𝔘 u (ü)		'uː (y)
V v	𝔙 v		fɑu
W w	𝔚 w		veː
X x	𝔛 ℨ		'iks
Y y	𝔜 ŋ		'ypsilɔn
Z z	ℨ ȝ		tsɛt

Note 4.—The double s is written ß (sz) at the end of a word or a syllable (when this syllable is not an integral part of the whole word but merely a prefix), and also after a long vowel and before a consonant:

muß, must   ißt, eats

eßbar, eatable, but essen, to eat

Fuß, foot   Kuß, kiss

Although the e in eßbar is short, the double s is written ß because at the end of a syllable, bar not being an integral part of the word, but an adjectival or adverbial suffix (-able).

In Fuß and Kuß, the u in the former is long and in the latter short, but both have ß because this is, as the above rule said, at the end of the word—*but* in the plural we have:

Füße (the double s not at the end but following a *long vowel*),

Küsse (not ß because the vowel ü is short in this word, and the double s is not now at the end).

Observations.—In writing German with Roman characters the student may write Füße (as most Germans do), or Füsse, but if he keeps to the former, it will help to keep his pronunciation correct, *i.e.* to remember that the preceding vowel is long. There is no rule we can give for helping the student to know whether the vowel before a final ß in nouns is long or short. He must learn this by experience.

Note carefully these printed capital letters, which beginners are apt to confuse:

B (B) and V (V)

C (C), G (G) and S (S)

R (R) and K (K)

O (O) and Q (Q)

Also f (f) and ſ (s) (the f has the stroke right across, whereas the ſ has not).

Note carefully: b (b), d (d) and ħ (h).

§ 2. GERMAN PRONUNCIATION

Preliminary Note

Before we go any further we must explain that the *symbols* we are using here to indicate the pronunciation are *symbols only and not ordinary German letters*. These symbols have been devised by the International Phonetic Association so that the pronunciation of all languages can be clearly explained by this International *Pronouncing* Alphabet. If you take the trouble to learn the sound-values of these symbols now you will be able to follow the phonetic transcription of any other language you undertake.

Practise your sounds aloud, clearly and continuously, and use a mirror to get your lip positions as indicated here.

A good pronunciation is well worth acquiring, and there is no reason why the average student who follows these notes conscientiously and continuously should not achieve this, although if he can obtain the help of a native or a good gramophone record on German pronunciation so much the better.

A Table of the Vowel-Sounds in German

Letter and Symbol	Nearest English Equivalent	Remarks
a $\begin{cases} \text{ɑ (long)}[1] \\ \text{ɑ (short)} \end{cases}$	*a* as in *father* *a* as in *cast* said quickly: not as in *cat*	Almost like *u* in *must*.

[1] A long vowel is indicated in the pronunciation by a colon (:).

Table of the Vowel-Sounds in German—*continued*

Letter and Symbol	Nearest English Equivalent	Remarks
e ɛ (long)	*ai* as in *fair*	There is no *er* sound at the end: it is one pure vowel-sound.
e ɛ (short)	*e* as in *bed, net, sent*	
e e (long)	*ee* as in *deep*	The teeth are not so close together as in the English *deep*. It is between the *ee* in *deep* and the *e* in *bed*.
e e (short)		As the preceding sound, but shorter.
i ɪ (always short)	*i* as in *bit*	
i i (long)	*ee* as in *deep*	The teeth are much closer together than in the English sound. The sound must almost be forced through.
o ɔ (always short)	*o* as in *not*	Morgen (mɔrgən)—*not* as in English Morgan.
o o (always long)	*aw* as in *lawn*	With lips *well rounded*. There is not the *o-oo* sound as in *bone*.
u { u (long)	*oo* as in *ooze*	Lips *well rounded!*
u { ʊ (short)	*oo* as in *good*	Lips *well rounded!*
ö œ (always short)	*ur* as in *fur* (*r* not being pronounced)	Lips *must be well rounded*, as for ɔ.
ö ø (always long)	No equivalent in English. It is the same as the French *eu* in *feu*	Pronounce the preceding sound, closing the mouth somewhat and keeping the lips rounded as for o.
ü y (long)	No equivalent in English. Almost like the French *u* as in *sur*	Put your lips as for whistling (position as for u) and try to say *ee*. The German grün (gryn) is like the English *green* with the lips kept as for whistling.
ü ʏ (short)	No English equivalent	As the preceding sound, but *short*. The German Müller is like the English *miller* with the lips as for whistling.
e ə	*a* as in *ago*, *er* as in *further*	A short sound, that of unaccented e.

Table of the Consonant-Sounds in German

Where no note is given the reader is to assume that the German consonant has the same sound as in English.

Letter and Symbol	Nearest English Equivalent	Remarks
b b	*b* as in *bed*	
b p	*p* as in *put*	Only when *b* stands at end of word or syllable.
c ts		ts pronounced as one sound: practise the "English" *that's 'im!* This is the sound of c before e, i, ö or ä. Has largely given way to *z*.
c k		The sound of c otherwise, although has largely given way to k.
ch k		In words from the Greek (Charakter).
ch ç	*h* in *huge*	Exaggerate the *h* in *huge*. Force the tongue against roof of mouth.
ch x	Scots *loch*	Whereas ç is pronounced at front of mouth, x is pronounced in the throat. Say *lock* forcing the air through on the *k*. This is the pronunciation of ch only after a, o, u or au.
d d	*d* as in *dead*	
d t	*t* as in *tomb*	This is the pronunciation of d at end of word or syllable.
g g	*g* as in *go*	Always, except as under.
g ʒ	*s* as in *casual*	Only in a few French words (Courage, kurɑːʒə).
g k		At end of word or syllable except when preceded by n: Tag (tɑk).
g ç		In -ig, except when followed by -lich: Sonnig (zɔnɪç), but: Königlich (kønɪglɪç).
h h	*h* as in *hand*	*Always* pronounced before a vowel.

Table of Consonant-Sounds in German—*continued*

Letter and Symbol	Nearest English Equivalent	Remarks
j j	*y* as in *yes*	
l l	*l* as in *lump*	Put tip of tongue between top teeth and gum.
ng ŋ	*ng* as in *sing*	Always: never pronounce *g* as in *finger*.
ph f		In words from Greek. Mostly replaced now by f.
qu kv		Quelle (kvɛlə).
r r		Is trilled more than in English, although scarcely heard in ending -er.
s s	*s* as in *soap*	At end of word or syllable only: Glas (glɑːs).
s z	*z* as in *zeal*	Only at beginning of word or syllable: Seife (zaifə), Rose (roːzə).
S s ʃ	*sh* as in *sharp*	Before p or t only: Speise (ʃpaizə), Stern (ʃtɛrn), sparen (ʃpɑːrən).
ss (ß) s	*s* as in *soap*	
sch ʃ	*sh* as in *sharp*	
v f	*f* as in *far*	Except in a few French words (Vase, vɑːzə).
w v	*v* as in *vat*	
y j	*y* as in *yes*	Only when a consonant: Yukka (jʊkɑ).
y { y (short) / y (long) / i		Does not often occur as a vowel.
z ts		See c above; z is always so pronounced.

Observations.—There are no silent letters as in English. Thus, although we say *knave*, the Germans say Knabe (knɑːbə), both the k and the e being pronounced.

h is not pronounced between two vowels unless the h is part of the following syllable: sehen (zeən), but: Hoheit (hohait).

chs when part of the word itself (the s not being added for some grammatical reason) is pronounced ks: sechs (zɛks), Ochs (ɔks), wachsen (vɑksən), etc.

The Glottal Stop is what the phoneticians mean by the forced stop between one word or syllable and a following one beginning with an accented or stressed vowel. Let us consider the English expression *fresh eggs*. We carry the *sh* sound straight on: fresheggs. But the equivalent German expression is not so pronounced. There is a pause after frische, the vocal organs contract, and the following word begins after a complete break between the two with an almost explosive force: frische Eier.

This is not entirely unknown in English. A Cockney will sometimes say, for instance, *Git aht o' 'ere*, the expression not being smoothly carried on, but rather awkwardly broken up.

The Glottal Stop is written phonetically.

The Stress in German

The German spoken language is strongly stressed. You have only to listen in to a German broadcast to realize that. The following rules will be more helpful later on, but in the meantime the stress will be indicated by a mark ′ after the stressed syllable.

1. The stress is laid on the *stem* of the word:

geh′-en, ge-fähr′-lich, Mäd′-chen

(The principal parts in these words being geh, fähr, Mäd.)

2. In compound words the stress is usually on the first part:

Turm′-uhr, eis′-kalt, Va′ter-land

But not with the adverbial particles: hin-ein′, da-mit′, etc.

3. Separable prefixes take the main stress:

aus′-gehen, hin-auf′-klettern, her-un′ter-kommen

4. The negative prefix un- is always stressed:

un'-artig, Un'-sinn, un'-erwartet

A Simple Exercise in Reading

The following passage is given first in Roman type, next in German Fraktur type, thirdly in phonetic script, and finally in literal English.

Practise the pronunciation carefully, referring constantly to the foregoing notes.

Roman Type

Der Winter ist kalt. Es regnet oft und es schneit manchmal. Dann sind die Dächer der Häuser mit Schnee bedeckt. Der Schnee ist weiß und schön. Die Jungen und Mädchen spielen gern mit dem Schnee. Manchmal sind die Flüsse und Teiche zugefroren. Dann nehmen die jungen Leute ihre Schlittschuhe und gehen auf das Eis. Dort haben sie viel Spaß. Wenn aber das Tauwetter eintritt, ist es gefährlich, auf das Eis zu gehen.

German Fraktur

Der Winter ist kalt. Es regnet oft und es schneit manchmal. Dann sind die Dächer der Häuser mit Schnee bedeckt. Der Schnee ist weiß und schön. Die Jungen und Mädchen spielen gern mit dem Schnee. Manchmal sind die Flüsse und Teiche zugefroren. Dann nehmen die jungen Leute ihre Schlittschuhe und gehen auf das Eis. Dort haben sie viel Spaß. Wenn aber das Tauwetter eintritt, ist es gefährlich, auf das Eis zu gehen.

Phonetic Version

dɛr vɪn'tər ʔɪst kalt. ɛs reg'nət ɔft ʔʊnt ʔɛs ʃnait manç'maːl. dan zɪnt di dɛ'çər dɛr hɔi'zər mɪt ʃneː bədɛkt'. dɛr ʃneː ʔɪst vais ʊnt ʃøːn. di jʊ'ŋən ʔʊnt mɛt'çən ʃpiː'lən gɛrn mɪt dɛm ʃneː. manç'maːl zɪnt di flʏ'sə ʔʊnt tai'çə tsu'gəfroˈrən. dan ne'ːmən di jʊ'ŋən bɔi'tə iːrə ʃlɪt'ʃuːə ʔʊnt ge'ːən auf das ʔais. dɔrt haˈ'ːbən zi fiːl ʃpaːs. vɛn ˀaːbər das tau'wɛtər ˀaintrɪt, ˀɪst ˀɛs gəfɛːr'lɪç, auf das ˀais tsu ge'ːən.

The following is given as a rough guide, although the student, if he seriously wishes to acquire a good pronunciation, must read and re-read the foregoing rules, and practise continually the previous phonetic version:

dair vinter ist kahlt. es reegnert (ert *very short!*) oft unt (u *as oo in book, not as u in but*) es shnite (*to rhyme with kite*) man-Hmahl. dahnn zint dee decher (deHer, H *as in huge*) dair hoyzer mit shnee berdeckt (ber *very short!*). dair shnee ist vice unt shern (*lips rounded!*). dee yungen unt met-Hern (ern *very short!*) shpeelern (ern *very short!*) gairn mit dem shnee. man-Hmahl zint die flisser (i *pronounced with rounded lips!*) unt tie-Her tsoogefroren (*stress on* tsoo *and* fror). Etc.

English Version

The winter is cold. It rains often and snows sometimes. Then are the roofs of-the houses with snow covered. The snow is white and beautiful. The boys and girls play gladly with the snow. Sometimes are the rivers and ponds over-frozen. Then take the young people their skates and go on-to the ice. There have they much fun. When the thaw-weather in-steps (sets in), is it dangerous on the ice to go.

LESSON I

THE SIMPLE SENTENCE

I. The Masculine Nouns

We now come to the study of the language itself. The name of any person or thing is called a noun. Thus *apple* and *tailor* are nouns.

Apple is singular, *apples* is plural.

The plural of nouns in German is formed in different ways. After all, we have, in addition to *apple, apples*, such plurals as *ox, oxen, man, men, woman, women, sheep, sheep, child, children*. We see in some of these plurals a change of vowel sound: *man, men; woman* (wʊmən), *women* (wɪmɪn), etc. This change of vowel sound, or Umlaut, as the Germans call it, occurs in the plural of many German nouns, but not all.

All German nouns, whether representing persons or things, are *masculine, feminine* or *neuter*, whereas in English things are usually neuter, although we often say *she* of a ship and other things. The *gender*, or sex, as it were, of a noun is very important, as the word for *the* (which is always the same in English) changes according to the gender. The student must therefore learn every noun with the article (*the*) before it. Thus it is not only necessary to know that *apple* is Apfel in German: he must know it is der Apfel.

In this first section we are going to deal only with masculine nouns ending in -el, -en or -er.

In the following list notice which nouns have the Umlaut in the plural and which have not. Notice also that the plural form of der (*the*) is die.

Notice further that *all nouns* are written with a capital letter in German.

Singular	Plural
der Vogel, bird	die Vögel
der Garten, garden	die Gärten
der Apfel, apple	die Äpfel
der Schneider, tailor	die Schneider
der Bruder, brother	die Brüder
der Vater, father	die Väter
der Lehrer, teacher	die Lehrer
der Schüler, schoolboy	die Schüler
der Onkel, uncle	die Onkel
der Bäcker, baker	die Bäcker
der Laden, shop	die Läden
der Wagen, cart, carriage, motor-car	die Wagen
der Fleischer, butcher	die Fleischer

Notice that Schneider, Lehrer and Fleischer have no Umlaut in the plural because e's and i's cannot take one. Of the others only Onkel and Wagen have no Umlaut in the plural, and Schüler and Bäcker have the Umlaut already in the singular.

Vocabulary

er, he	schön, beautiful
sie, they	ehrlich, honest
ist, is	unehrlich, dishonest
sind, are	ja, yes
nicht, not	nein, no
dort, there	manchmal, sometimes
hier, here	immer, always
gut, good	oft, often
schlecht, bad	freundlich, friendly, kind
arm, poor	böse, angry, wicked
reich, rich	sehr, very

Exercise 1

Read and then turn into English:

Der Bruder ist arm. Der Vater ist nicht böse. Ist der Onkel hier? Nein, er ist dort. Ist der Laden nicht hier? Ja, er[1] ist hier. Der Bäcker ist oft unehrlich. Der Schüler ist manchmal böse. Ist der Apfel nicht gut? Nein, er ist schlecht. Ist der Garten schön?

---

[1] Note that, as these words are masculine, even though some of them refer to things the English *it* must in all these cases become er (*he*) in German.

Ja, er ist schön. Ist der Lehrer immer freundlich? Nein, er ist manchmal böse. Ist der Onkel arm? Nein, er ist sehr reich.

Exercise 2

Turn the above sentences into the plural. Remember that the adjective after the verb *is* or *are* does not change. We will show you by doing the first one: Die Brüder sind arm. When you have completed the exercise (but not before) turn to the Key beginning page 149 and see whether you have made any mistakes.

2. The Feminine Nouns

We are now going to deal with a number of feminine monosyllables (words of one syllable). Notice that the word for *the* is die in both the singular and the plural. All these words have the Umlaut in the plural (except where the vowel is e or i) and take -e as their plural ending:

Singular	Plural
die Stadt, city, town	die Städte
die Nacht, night	die Nächte
die Hand, hand	die Hände
die Kuh, cow	die Kühe
die Magd, maid	die Mägde
die Maus, mouse	die Mäuse
die Nuß, nut	die Nüsse
die Wand, wall	die Wände
die Wurst, sausage	die Würste
die Gans, goose	die Gänse

Vocabulary

dunkel, dark	klein, little, short
schwarz, black	dick, fat, thick
braun, brown	ganz, quite
weiß, white	dünn, thin
fertig, ready	hungrig, hungry
sie, she, they	durstig, thirsty
reif, ripe	alt, old
sauer, sour	neu, new
groß, big, tall	und, and

Exercise 3

Read and then turn into English:

Die Stadt ist sehr alt. Ist die Nuß reif? Die Kuh ist nicht braun. Die Gans ist nicht sehr groß. Ist die Nacht nicht dunkel? Ist die Wurst fertig? Die Wand ist sehr dünn. Ist die Hand braun? Nein, sie ist weiß. Ist die Kuh durstig? Nein, sie ist hungrig. Die Stadt ist nicht alt, sie ist neu. Ist die Maus immer klein? Die Magd ist manchmal sehr freundlich. Die Nuß ist alt und sauer. Die Nacht ist ganz schwarz. Der Bäcker ist klein und dick.

Exercise 4

Turn the above exercise into the plural, afterwards comparing it with the answers in the Key (see page 149).

3. The Neuter Nouns

Now we come to the third and last gender. *Neuter* is a Latin word meaning *neither, i.e.* neither masculine nor feminine. Notice that in this case the singular definite article is das (*the*), while the plural is, as for the masculine and feminine, again die. These neuter nouns we give here all take the Umlaut in the plural (except where the vowel is e or i) and the plural ending is -er.

Singular	Plural
das Blatt, leaf	die Blätter
das Buch, book	die Bücher
das Dach, roof	die Dächer
das Dorf, village	die Dörfer
das Ei, egg	die Eier
das Feld, field	die Felder
das Glas, glass	die Gläser
das Haus, house	die Häuser
das Horn, horn	die Hörner
das Kind, child	die Kinder
das Kleid, dress	die Kleider
das Lied, song	die Lieder
das Rad, wheel	die Räder
das Wort, word	die Wörter

Vocabulary

lang, long	viereckig, square
kurz, short	hoch, high
voll, full	niedrig, low
leer, empty	aber, but
grün, green	oder, or
rot, red	ziemlich, fairly
es, it	fast, almost, nearly
schwer, difficult, heavy	zu, too
leicht, easy	selten, seldom
rund, round	jetzt, now

Exercise 5

Read and then translate into English:

Das Lied ist nicht sehr schön. Das Rad ist rund. Ist das Dorf nicht klein und sehr alt? Das Ei ist nicht rund. Das Dach ist rot. Das Buch ist nicht zu schwer. Ist das Glas nicht leer? Nein, es ist fast zu voll. Ist das Wort leicht? Nein, es ist sehr lang und schwer. Ist das Kind groß? Nein, es ist sehr klein. Das Haus ist ziemlich hoch. Ist das Feld rund oder viereckig? Es ist viereckig. Das Kleid ist ganz neu, aber es ist nicht sehr schön. Das Blatt ist lang und grün. Ist das Haus nicht zu niedrig?

Exercise 6

Turn the above exercise into the plural, and then compare your answers with the Key.

Revision Exercise

Translate into German:

Are the gardens long and beautiful? They are beautiful, but they are not very long. Is the tailor always honest? Yes, he is always honest. Is the glass always full? No, it is often empty. Are the cities old or new? They are old. The fields are nearly always green. Are the nuts not ripe? The apples are too green and sour.

Is the house big or small?   It is very big.   Are the shops
always empty?   No, they are seldom empty.   Are the
schoolboys tall and thin?   No, they are short and fat.
Are the children always good?   No, they are sometimes
very wicked.   The night is long and very dark.   The
brother is poor but honest, and the father is rich but
dishonest.   The songs are too long and too difficult.
Here is the village, and there is the house.   The child is
nearly always hungry.

LESSON II

THE WEAK VERB

Pronouns are little words which are used to avoid the
repetition of nouns, and a few English pronouns are:
I, you, we, us, them, it.

Pronouns are divided into persons and numbers.
There are three persons:

First person: the person speaking (*I, we, me, us*).
Second person: the person addressed (*you*).
Third person: the person spoken about (*he, she, it,
    they, him, her, them*).

The numbers are singular (one person, as *I, you, he,
she, it*) and plural (as *we, you, they*).

As in English we must say *I am, he is, we are*, and it is
wrong to say *we is, he am, they loves*, etc., so in German
there are certain endings to the verb (the word which
expresses a *state* or an *action*, as *am, do, love, hate*, etc.)
and these endings must be learnt carefully by heart, and
must never be confused.

Let us look at the following conjugation, or arrange-
ment of the verb:

lieben, to love

Singular		Plural	
ich liebe	I love	wir lieben	we love
du liebst	you love	ihr liebt	you love
er ⎫	he ⎫		
sie ⎬ liebt	she ⎬ loves	sie lieben	they love
es ⎭	it ⎭		
Sie lieben	you love	Sie lieben	you love

First of all, let us explain the various forms meaning *you love*.

Du is used to one person with whom one is very friendly and intimate. It is also used by grown-ups to a young child, and it is used always to address an animal. It may also be used to express contempt. Du is only written with a capital letter in correspondence.

Ihr is the form used in the above circumstances when more than one person, child or animal is being addressed.

Sie (always written with a capital) is used in all other cases. It is the ordinary form of address, and the only one likely to be used by the average English person just staying in Germany for a short time. He may use du to a small child or a dog, but let him beware of using du to anybody else! Sie means *you* whether one person only is addressed or several, and the verb ending (-en) is the same in both cases.

The one who is something or does something is called the *subject*. When the subject is a noun the verb has the same ending as after the pronouns *he* or *they*:

Der Bruder ⎫ liebt	The brother ⎫ loves
Er ⎭	He ⎭
Die Brüder ⎫ lieben	The brothers ⎫ love
Sie ⎭	They ⎭

The student must therefore see that his verb ending is the correct one for the subject: thus in the verb lieben, to love, to the stem lieb- are added endings as follows:

ich has the verb ending in -e   –   ich liebe
du   ,,   ,,   ,,   -st (-est) *du liebst

er		er liebt
sie		sie liebt
es	have the verb ending in -t (-et)*	es liebt
ihr		ihr liebt
wir		wir lieben
sie	,, ,, ,, -en	sie lieben
Sie		Sie lieben

Note.—With the -st (-est) and -t (-et) endings the extra e is put in when the *stem* of the verb (*i.e.* that part left when the endings are taken away) ends in a consonant followed by d, t, m or n, in the du, er and ihr forms. When the stem ends in a hissing consonant (s, z, ss, ß), the extra e may be put in the du form, or, particularly in spoken German, the du form may become like the er form.

Examples (using the verbs öffnen, landen, atmen, zeichnen, reisen, tanzen):

du öffnest (you open), er landet (he lands), du atmest (you breathe), er zeichnet (he draws);

du reis(es)t (you travel), er reist (he travels);

du tanz(es)t (you dance), ihr tanzt (you dance)

Notice further that verbs whose infinitive (or simplest) form ends in -ern or -eln have -ere and -le after ich, and -ert and -elt after er or ihr:

ändern, to change:

ich ändere,	I change
du änderst,	you change
er ändert,	he changes

lächeln, to smile:

ich lächle,	I smile
du lächelst,	you smile
er lächelt,	he smiles

Asking a Question

The interrogative form is quite simple. The English *do* or *does* in such forms as *Do I smoke? Does she dance? Do you telephone? Does the man travel?* do not exist in German. The German question form is always *Smoke I? Dances she? Telephone you? Travels the man?* etc. Thus:

Do I smoke?	Rauche ich?
Does she dance?	Tanzt sie?
Do you telephone?	Telefonieren Sie?
Does the man travel?	Reist der Mann?

The Negative Form

We also use *do* and *does* in making a negative state-ment. The Germans never do this, but say quite simply *I smoke not, she dances not,* etc.

I do not smoke.	Ich rauche nicht.
She does not dance.	Sie tanzt nicht.
You do not telephone.	Sie telefonieren nicht.
The man does not travel.	Der Mann reist nicht.

Vocabulary

träumen, to dream	kochen, to boil
atmen, to breathe	spielen, to play
reisen, to travel	sagen, to say
zeichnen, to draw	antworten, to answer
lieben, to love	lachen, to laugh
hassen, to hate	lächeln, to smile
schicken, to send	suchen, to seek, look for
telefonieren, to telephone	hören, to hear
rauchen, to smoke	weinen, to weep
arbeiten, to work	besuchen, to visit
reichen, to hand, pass	pflücken, to pick, gather
öffnen, to open	zeigen, to show
machen, to make	

Exercise 7

Put the following into the plural, thus:

Ich träume	wir träumen
Du tanz(es)t	ihr tanzt
Er raucht	sie rauchen
Der Schneider arbeitet	die Schneider arbeiten

Ich besuche. Du suchst. Er sagt. Telefoniert sie?
Der Bruder lacht. Der Vater raucht. Spielt der
Schüler? Du sagst. Ich höre. Sie haßt. Sie (you)
suchen.

Exercise 8

Put the following into the singular:

Träumen wir? Ihr antwortet. Sie (they, masc.) zeichnen. Die Onkel reisen. Die Kinder atmen. Hören Sie (you)? Sie (they, fem.) arbeiten. Die Brüder hassen. Wir lächeln. Antworten die Lehrer?

Exercise 9

Translate into German:

(a) I hear the cow. The uncle opens the book. The maids boil the sausages. We are not laughing[1]. You (du, *or 2nd sing.*) look for the nuts. The tailors make the dresses. The brother visits the village. I pass the glasses. The children hate the song. She draws the house. I smile, but she weeps.

(b) We look for the cows. I hear the mice. Do you (Sie) send the books? Does she smoke? Do you (Sie) not dance? Does the father work? Do the children play? Is the maid boiling[1] the eggs? Am I dreaming? Are you (*2nd sing.*) weeping? Is the child breathing?

LESSON III

THE CASES

We said before that the person or thing which is or does something is the *Subject*. The *Subject* is always in what is called the *Nominative Case*. This is so in English, but it does not matter much to us, as our words do not change much, but it is important in German.

When the action of the verb passes directly on to

---

[1] I am working = I work.
Am I working? = work I?

somebody or something else, that somebody or something
is the *Direct Object*, and is in the *Accusative Case*.

If we take the sentence *The tailor makes the dress*, and
ask: *Who makes the dress?* we get the answer *The tailor*.
The tailor is there the Subject and in the Nominative
Case.   If we ask: *What does he make?* we get the answer
The dress.   The dress is therefore the Direct Object, in
the Accusative Case.

In Exercise 9 we successfully did a number of sentences
like this without needing to know anything about cases.
But that was because the sentences were carefully chosen
to avoid difficulties.   If you go back to that exercise
you will find that no masculine singular nouns occurred
in the Direct Object or Accusative Case, because der
(Nominative singular) becomes den (Accusative singular),
although the feminine singular, neuter singular and the
plural forms (die, das and die) remain the same.

We will now do an exercise including some masculine
singular nouns in the Accusative Case.   Compare the
following:

> Der Bruder arbeitet
> Ich besuche den Bruder.

In the first sentence, who works?   The brother—
therefore the Nominative Case.

In the second sentence, whom do I visit?   The brother
—therefore in the Accusative.   ·

Exercise 10

Besuchst du den Onkel?   Ich suche die Eier.   Der
Bruder besucht den Laden.   Der Schneider reicht das
Kleid.   Der Lehrer sucht den Schüler.   Wir hören die
Schüler.   Der Fleischer schickt die Würste.   Das Kind
pflückt den Apfel.   Es pflückt Äpfel.

THE CASES

Exercise 11

Do you[1] hear the song? I visit the butcher. We look for the teacher. The schoolboy looks for eggs. I draw the house. The teacher says the word. The father visits the uncle. She does not answer. Does the uncle visit the town? You (du) visit the baker.

There is another kind of object, the *Indirect Object*. This might be said to answer the question *To whom?* Consider the sentence:

The tailor sends the baker the apples.

Who sends?	The tailor.	(Nominative Case.)
What does he send?	The apples.	(Accusative Case.)
To whom does he send?	To the baker.	(Dative Case)

Very often the Dative Case is expressed in English by *to*: The tailor sends the apples to the baker. But as this *to* does not imply physical motion towards, but a receiving of something, the *to* is not expressed in German, the Dative Case of the article and the noun being sufficient.

The Dative Case of the Article is as follows:

Singular			Plural
Masc.	Fem.	Neut.	M., F. and N.
dem	der	dem	den

N.B. In the case of two nouns, the Dative precedes the Accusative, no matter what the English order may be.

Exercise 12

Der Onkel reicht dem Vater die Nüsse. Die Magd schickt dem Bruder die Äpfel. Der Vater antwortet[2] dem Schneider. Der Bäcker schickt dem Lehrer Nüsse und Äpfel. Du reichst dem Vater den Apfel. Wir

[1] Use Sie unless told differently.
[2] The meaning is: *replies to.*

schicken der Magd Bücher und Kleider. Ich reiche dem Kind das Ei.

Exercise 13

The teacher sends the father the book. The father passes the nuts to the uncle. The schoolboys hand the books to the teacher. We send eggs and apples to the maid. The schoolboy answers the father. The maid hands the dress to the tailor. I pass the glass to the baker. You answer the teacher.

Sometimes a noun is put next to another noun in a descriptive sense, to express ownership. Thus we say in English *the uncle's book* or *the book of the uncle*. The thing we are really talking about is the book, and we add *uncle's* or *of the uncle* to describe which book. The case of this expression *uncle's* or *of the uncle* is called Possessive in English, and in German it is referred to as the Genitive Case. The noun in the Genitive Case usually (but not always) follows the noun on which it depends, and the Definite Article is also put into the Genitive Case.

The Genitive Case of the Definite Article is as follows:

Singular			Plural
Masc.	Fem.	Neut.	M., F. and N.
des	der	des	der

Of the nouns that we have used up till now the *feminines take no ending* in the Genitive singular, the masculines in -el, -en, -er take s and the neuters take s or es. In the plural they all have the same endings as for the Nominative plural.

Masc. des Lehrers, of the teacher   der Lehrer, of the teachers
Fem. der Stadt, of the town   der Städte, of the towns
Neut. des Blattes, of the leaf   der Blätter, of the leaves

Position of nicht in the sentence

Nicht (*not*) is usually placed after the direct object, although in a question it often comes after the verb:

Er schickt die Äpfel nicht. He does not send the apples.
Schickt er nicht dem Bäcker die Äpfel? Does he not send the apples to the baker?

Exercise 14

Der Laden des Bäckers ist schön und neu. Die Kühe des Onkels sind groß und braun. Die Räder des Wagens sind rund. Das Kleid der Magd ist rot. Die Wände des Hauses sind weiß. Die Häuser der Dörfer sind klein. Das Glas des Kindes ist leer. Der Lehrer öffnet die Bücher der Schüler. Der Bruder des Schneiders zeigt dem Fleischer des Dorfes die Gans. Hörst du nicht die Lieder der Kinder? Ich telefoniere mit[1] dem Vater des Bäckers. Der Bruder des Schneiders schickt dem Kind des Bäckers Äpfel und Nüsse. Die Hörner der Kuh sind nicht sehr lang. Die Hände der Magd sind klein und weiß, aber die Hände der Brüder sind sehr groß und rot.

Exercise 15

Remember that of two noun objects, the Indirect (Dative) precedes the Direct (Accusative).

The horns of the cows are not too long. I telephone the brother of the maid. The roof of the house is square and red. The schoolboy's father answers the teacher. The uncle sends eggs and apples to the tailor's brother. Does he not visit the tailor of the village? Do you not hear the bird's song? The bakers' shops are quite full. The baker's brother hears the songs of the children. I do not send the maid's dress to the tailor.

[1] To telephone someone, telefonieren mit (*with*) + Dative.

LESSON IV

HABEN, SEIN AND THE IMPERFECT

Nearly all masculine nouns ending in e form all their cases except the Nominative sing. by simply adding n. Thus der Knabe, the boy:

	Singular	Plural
Nom.	der Knabe	die Knaben
Acc.	den Knaben	die Knaben
Gen.	des Knaben	der Knaben
Dat.	dem Knaben	den Knaben

Note that there is no Umlaut.

There are two verbs that you cannot learn too soon or too well. Here they are: haben, to have, and sein, to be.

Present of haben

	Singular		Plural	
1.	ich habe	I have	wir haben	we have
2.	du hast	thou hast	{ Sie haben / ihr habt }	you have
3.	er hat	he has	sie haben	they have

Observe that haben is a little irregular so far as we know it yet. Sein is quite irregular.

Present of sein

	Singular		Plural	
1.	ich bin	I am	wir sind	we are
2.	du bist	thou art	{ Sie sind / ihr seid }	you are
3.	er ist	he is	sie sind	they are

So far we have been dealing with the *Present tense*, that is, our verbs have dealt only with things now going on. In dealing with things that were done in the past we use a form of verb called the *Imperfect tense*. It is easily learned, and differs from the Present in having a t all through, and in having a final e in the third person singular. Compare the following with the Present of lieben as given on page 28:

Imperfect Indicative of lieben

Singular		Plural	
1. ich liebte	I loved	wir liebten	we loved
2. du liebtest	thou lovedst	Sie liebten / ihr liebtet	you loved
3. er liebte	he loved	sie liebten	they loved

The Imperfect may be put into English in two ways:
(1) *I loved*, (2) *I was loving*. Ich liebte does duty for
both forms. In English we often use *do* and *is*, and *was*
and *did* along with verbs. *I am loving, you were loving*,
etc., are called the *progressive* form, because they show
that the loving is or was going on continuously: *I do love,
she did love*, etc., are called the emphatic form. But
German does not allow this use of *am, was, do, did*; these
little words are NEVER put into German along with verbs.
I do love is just ich liebe. I am loving is just the same,
ich liebe. Do I love? = liebe ich? Am I loving? is the
same, liebe ich? I was loving = ich liebte. I did
love = ich liebte. Did I love? = liebte ich? She is
loving = sie liebt. Does she love? = liebt sie?

Vocabulary

der Neffe, nephew	leben, to live, be alive
der Löwe, lion	lernen, to learn
der Franzose, Frenchman	erzählen, to tell, relate
der Hase, hare	wohnen, to dwell, live
der Ochse, ox	wo? where?
der Matrose, sailor	oben, upstairs
der Junge, boy	unten, downstairs
tot, dead	noch, still

Exercise 16

Wir sind Franzosen. Wo wohnen die Brüder des
Matrosen? Sie wohnen nicht hier. Erzähltest du dem
Jungen das Lied der Matrosen? Sind die Neffen des
Franzosen oben? Nein, sie sind unten. Leben die
Brüder des Knaben? Nein, sie sind tot. Die Jungen
zeichneten die Löwen. Lernten Sie nicht das Lied des
Matrosen? Wir besuchten nicht oft den Neffen des

Franzosen. Die Hörner des Ochsen sind sehr lang. Sie schickten den Matrosen Äpfel, Nüsse und Eier.

Exercise 17

Where do you live? Does the hare still live (= live still)? No, it is dead. Did you send the boy's book to the baker's nephew? Where is the sailor's house? It is there. Where are the Frenchman's oxen? They are not here. Is not the Frenchmen's house white? No, it is red; there is the roof of the house. Is the sailor's nephew not learning the song? Was the Frenchman's nephew smoking? No, he was not smoking, he was working. Are the sailor's children playing? I was laughing, but she was weeping. Did you live upstairs or downstairs?

Exercise 18

We are poor, but you are rich. Marie is upstairs and Peter is playing downstairs. Gretchen and Paula have the hare. It is big and brown. Has the sailor the ox? Are you (du) still there? Yes, I am here. Have the sailors glasses? Yes, they have glasses, but they are empty. Where are we? We are upstairs. Where are the sailor's nephews playing? They are there. Have you (du) cows and oxen? No, they are dead.

Conversational Expressions

Guten Morgen!	Good morning!
Guten Abend!	Good evening!
Guten Tag!	Good day!
Gute Nacht!	Good night!
Wie geht es Ihnen?	How are you?
Sehr gut, danke, und Ihnen?	Very well, thank you, and you?

LESSON V

THE DEMONSTRATIVE ADJECTIVES—SOME PREPOSITIONS

Imperfect of sein

Singular		Plural	
1. ich war	I was	wir waren	we were
2. du warst	thou wast	Sie waren / ihr wart	you were
3. er war	he was	sie waren	they were

Imperfect of haben

Singular		Plural	
1. ich hatte	I had	wir hatten	we had
2. du hattest	thou hadst	Sie hatten / ihr hattet	you had
3. er hatte	he had	sie hatten	they had

Exercise 19

Die Nüsse und Äpfel waren nicht reif. Der Neffe des Lehrers war oben. Die Brüder der Magd waren tot. Die Kühe des Onkels waren groß und braun. Ich hatte den Hasen, aber er ist tot. War der Vater des Schülers sehr böse? Nein, er war ziemlich freundlich. War das Glas des Matrosen leer? Nein, es war ganz voll. Hattest du den Garten? Ja, er war sehr schön. Wo warst du? Ich war oben.

Exercise 20

Where was the sailor? He was not here. Were the teachers there? Yes, and the scholars. Was the teacher always friendly? No, he was often very angry. Did you have the house there? Yes, we had the house and the garden. Were the sausages ready? No, but we had apples and nuts. I was very thirsty and the glass was quite empty.

The Definite Article and the Demonstratives

It is better to learn the article, as you have been doing, by using it. But since we have now seen it in all its forms, it may be well to gather it up into one table for reference.

	Singular			Plural
	Masc.	Fem.	Neut.	M., F. and N.
Nom.	der	die	das	die
Acc.	den	die	das	die
Gen.	des	der	des	der
Dat.	dem	der	dem	den

There is another reason for giving the article in full here. There are certain little words called *demonstratives* that are used to point out nouns in German, and these are declined exactly like der, die, das. These words are dieser = this; jener[1] = that; jeder = every. With the three genders they appear:

Singular			Plural
Masc.	Fem.	Neut.	M., F. and N.
dieser	diese	dieses	diese
jener	jene	jenes	jene
jeder	jede	jedes	alle

The very meaning of the word shows us that we cannot have a plural of jeder; we use alle instead. We cannot say *every houses*, but we can say *all houses*: alle Häuser.

Another word, which does not point out but asks a question, is declined in the same way. It is welcher, welche, welches (sing.), welche (plural). It means *which?*

Thus: dieser Ochse = this ox; jedes Buch = every book; welches Buch? = which book?

Some Prepositions

Prepositions are little words like *to, with* or *in*, which show the relation between certain words in sentences. In

---

[1] *Jener* is relatively rare, particularly in colloquial language, where the definite article is often used instead.

English prepositions are said to govern the Accusative Case, but in German they may govern the Accusative, the Dative or the Genitive Case. We shall begin with six which govern the *Dative*.

aus, out of	in,[1] in
mit, with	von, of or from
nach, after or to	zu, to or at

Thus we write: aus dem Hause = out of the house, in der Stadt = in the town, nach dem Lehrer = after the teacher, zu Hause = at the house or at home.

Vocabulary

eins, one	elf, eleven	der Krieg, war
zwei, two	zwölf, twelve	das Zimmer, room
drei, three	dreizehn, thirteen	die Kirche, church
vier, four	vierzehn, fourteen	das Geschäft, business
fünf, five	fünfzehn, fifteen	die Schule, school
sechs, six	sechzehn, sixteen	die Klasse, class
sieben, seven	siebzehn, seventeen	es war, there (it) was
acht, eight	achtzehn, eighteen	es waren, there were
neun, nine	neunzehn, nineteen	
zehn, ten	zwanzig, twenty	

Exercise 21

Welches Kind spielt in dem Garten? Dieses Kind spielt in dem Garten mit dem Neffen des Schneiders. Waren[2] zehn Kühe auf[3] dem Feld? Nein, es waren acht Ochsen dort. Jeder Schüler hatte vier Bücher. In welcher Klasse bist du? Ich bin in dieser Klasse. Waren Sie sehr arm nach dem Krieg? Der Bäcker schickte den Neffen aus dem Zimmer. In welchem Dorf wohnten Sie? Wir wohnten in diesem Dorf, in dem Haus dort.

---

[1] *In* can *also* govern the Accusative (Lesson XII).
[2] Notice that when war or waren comes first, the es is omitted.
[3] Auf (*on*) is used with Feld.

Exercise 22

Had every child five or six apples? Which teacher sent the father this book? The three children were in the church. I sent the children to (the) school. Were there eight or nine houses in the village? There were seven. There are (es sind) five teachers in this school, and there are ten children in each class. In which house do you live? Which song did you learn? Which boy did you send out of the class? Which cow did you hear? He sent nine eggs with the dress. Every child in this village has three or four books. In which room is the sailor's nephew? He is upstairs in the uncle's room.

Conversation

Bitte, reichen Sie mir den Hut!	Please pass me that hat.
Hier ist er.	Here it is.
Danke vielmals!	Many thanks.
Bitte schön.	Not at all.
Bitte, wo ist die Post?	Please, where is the Post Office?
In der Straße dort, links (rechts).	In that street on the left (right).
Auf Wiedersehen!	Good-bye!

LESSON VI

DECLENSION OF GERMAN NOUNS

We have hitherto dealt in detail only with three types of plurals of nouns:

der Lehrer	die Lehrer
die Nacht	die Nächte
das Dorf	die Dörfer

We are now going to ask the student, in his own interest, to learn by heart (and the sooner the better) the Table of Declensions given on pp. 185–187. If he does this he will have no difficulty in declining (or giving the different forms of) any noun he may come across. Learning these lists will also add to his vocabulary a number of very useful words of which he has need. Some teachers do not advise learning lists by heart, but it is much more important and useful than learning a few poems by heart, and the student should even then constantly refer to the Table and the lists. For instance, suppose he comes across a masculine monosyllable, say, der Kopf, *the head*. *Masculine monosyllables*, says the Table, have their plural in -e (except a few easily learnt by heart in List 5 on page 187) and some have the Umlaut in the plural, while others have not. The list of those which have not is given on page 186, and reference to that (until the whole list is known by heart) will show that der Kopf does not occur there. Therefore der Kopf has the Umlaut in the plural.

Similarly, he will notice that of the *Feminine* nouns, die Mutter and die Tochter only are in Declension 1 (both taking the Umlaut), there are about 30 in Declension 2 (all monosyllables and all taking the Umlaut in the plural), whereas all other feminine nouns (except those in -nis in Declension 2) are in Declension 4. There are *no feminines* in Declension 3, and the student must never forget that *no feminine noun has any ending in the singular*.

If the student has to deal with a *Neuter* monosyllable, he will refer to List 4 on page 187. If it occurs in that list it takes the Umlaut and ends in -er in the plural. If not it is in Declension 2, does not take any Umlaut in the plural and its plural ending is -e.

Notice particularly that there is *always an* -n *in the Dative plural* whether of nouns, articles or adjectives.

The brackets round the (e) in the Dative singular of

Declensions 2 and 3 mean that this e is not always added. It is added as a rule only in the case of monosyllables and need not be added even then.

The brackets round the (e) in Declension 4 mean that where the word already ends in -e or in a weak ending (-el, -en, -er) -n only is added.

We give here the full declension of the nouns indicated in the Table:

Declension 1

der Laden, shop		der Wagen, cart, car	
der Laden	die Läden	der Wagen	die Wagen
den Laden	die Läden	den Wagen	die Wagen
des Ladens	der Läden	des Wagens	der Wagen
dem Laden	den Läden	dem Wagen	den Wagen

Declension 2

Masculine

der Kopf, head		der Schuh, shoe	
der Kopf	die Köpfe	der Schuh	die Schuhe
den Kopf	die Köpfe	den Schuh	die Schuhe
des Kopfes	der Köpfe	des Schuhes	der Schuhe
dem Kopf(e)	den Köpfen	dem Schuh(e)	den Schuhen

Feminine   Neuter

die Nacht, night		das Schaf, sheep	
die Nacht	die Nächte	das Schaf	die Schafe
die Nacht	die Nächte	das Schaf	die Schafe
der Nacht	der Nächte	des Schafes	der Schafe
der Nacht	den Nächten	dem Schaf(e)	den Schafen

Declension 3

Neuter   Masculine

das Glas, glass		der Mann, man	
das Glas	die Gläser	der Mann	die Männer
das Glas	die Gläser	den Mann	die Männer
des Glases	der Gläser	des Mannes	der Männer
dem Glas(e)	den Gläsern	dem Mann(e)	den Männern

Declension 4

derivative

Feminine

III mixed

die Übung, exercise		die Schwester, sister	
die Übung	die Übungen	die Schwester	die Schwestern
die Übung	die Übungen	die Schwester	die Schwestern
der Übung	der Übungen	der Schwester	der Schwestern
der Übung	den Übungen	der Schwester	den Schwestern

II weak

Masculine

der Knabe, boy		der Student, student	
der Knabe	die Knaben	der Student	die Studenten
den Knaben	die Knaben	den Studenten	die Studenten
des Knaben	der Knaben	des Studenten	der Studenten
dem Knaben	den Knaben	dem Studenten	den Studenten

The Table of Declensions on pages 185–187 sums up in a nutshell the whole question of German Nouns, and it will be the student's own fault if he continues to be confused and disheartened by German plurals. The more he refers to those pages and the sooner he learns them by heart the better. They apply to 95 per cent. of the nouns in the German language.

Of the other 5 per cent. we may mention here those nouns in -or (from the Latin) with the stress in the syllable *before* the -or in the singular and on the -or in the plural. Such are der Direk'tor, der Dok'tor, der Profes'sor, etc.

der Profes'sor	die Professo'ren
den Profes'sor	die Professo'ren
des Profes'sors	der Professo'ren
dem Profes'sor	den Professo'ren

Finally there are a few modern words of foreign origin that have their plural in -s, such as das Auto, motor-car:

das Auto	die Autos
das Auto	die Autos
des Autos	der Autos
dem Auto	den Autos

It will be seen from the foregoing that the most important parts of a noun's declension are the Genitive

singular and the Nominative plural.   Constant practice
alone will lead to success.

Vocabulary

der Mantel, coat	die Uhr, clock, watch
das Fenster, window	die Taschenuhr,[1] pocket watch
die Tür, door	der Handschuh,[1] glove
der Stock, stick	das Haar, hair
die Socke, sock	das Bein, leg
der Hut, hat	das Licht, light
die Mütze, cap	der Tag, day
der Anzug,[1] suit	der Vogel, bird
der Knopf, button	die Brust, breast, chest
der Strumpf, stocking	der Kragen, collar

Exercise 23

Give the number (1, 2, 3, or 4) of the Declension, the
Genitive singular and the Nominative plural of the
nouns given in the preceding Vocabulary.   Thus:

der Mantel   1   des Mantels   die Mäntel

LESSON VII

INDEFINITE ARTICLE AND POSSESSIVE ADJECTIVES

In German as in English there are two articles, the
definite—which we now know pretty well—and the indefinite.   The indefinite article in English is *a* or *an*.   In
German it is ein or eine.   You had better learn it from
this table, which you will readily understand by comparing it with the table of the definite article.   Obviously
ein can have no plural.

[1] Notice that in the case of Compound Nouns it is the final or
main part which has the gender and declension.   For example,
in Anzug, Zug is a masculine monosyllable, An is a prefix.   Therefore der Anzug is declined as a masculine monosyllable.

	Masc.	Fem.	Neut.	
Nom.	ein	eine	ein	a (an *or* one)
Acc.	einen	eine	ein	a
Gen.	eines	einer	eines	of a
Dat.	einem	einer	einem	to a

You can readily trace a resemblance to the *endings* of the definite article, and this resemblance will make it easy for you to remember the declension.

There are certain other very important words *that go with nouns* and are declined exactly like ein, eine, ein—only they have a plural. These words are:

	Singular			Plural
	Masc.	Fem.	Neut.	All genders
thy	dein	deine	dein	deine
your {	Ihr	Ihre	Ihr	Ihre
	euer	eure[1]	euer	eure[1]
her, their *or* its	ihr	ihre	ihr	ihre
no (*with a noun*)	kein	keine	kein	keine
my	mein	meine	mein	meine
his *or* its	sein	seine	sein	seine
our	unser	unsere	unser	unsere

Observe that the only difference between ihr (her, its or their) and Ihr (your) is the capital letter. The plurals of the above words have the same endings as the plural of der. Thus:

Nom.	die (the)	-e	deine (thy)	ihre (her, their or its)
Acc.	die	-e	deine	ihre
Gen.	der	-er	deiner	ihrer
Dat.	den	-en	deinen	ihren

There are really *three* ways in German of expressing the English word *your*. If we are speaking of one person with whom we are familiar, we say dein as above. If we are speaking of more than one person with whom we are familiar, we use euer (m.), eure (f.), euer (n.), eure (pl.). Then there is the ordinary polite form—which is the form for us—Ihr, Ihre, Ihr, Ihre.

---

[1] Note the disappearance of the second e.

Declension of Proper Nouns

Names of individual persons and places are called proper nouns. In German it is getting more and more unusual to decline proper nouns. Karl (Charles) might be treated as a Kopf noun, but as a matter of fact the only case in which it changes is the Genitive: Karls Buch = *Charles's book*. This is clearly just the same as in English. But if we want to use the Dative or Accusative of a proper noun we *may* indicate this by the article which shows which case we mean. To Socrates = dem Sokrates. He saw Jason = er sah den Jason. But this is mainly used with classical names, or colloquially.

To express the Possessive case of proper names ending in a hissing consonant the Germans use -ens: Maxens Buch = *Max's book*. However the use of von is preferred: Max's shoes = die Schuhe von Max.

The names of places (countries, towns, etc.) are usually neuter, and take no article. They form their Genitive by von or by the Genitive -s:

> Die Hauptstadt von Deutschland (die Hauptstadt Deutschlands) ist Berlin, the capital of Germany is Berlin.

Feminine names of countries (die Schweiz, Switzerland, die Türkei, etc.) *do* require the article:

> Die Hauptstadt der Schweiz, the capital of Switzerland.

Notice that we say die Stadt Berlin, die Universität London, not: die Stadt von Berlin, etc.

-er may be added to names of towns to indicate the inhabitant, or to form an adjective:

> Die Berliner sagen das nicht, the Berliners do not say that.
> In einer Londoner Zeitung, in a London newspaper.
> Pilsener Bier, Pilsen Beer.

Vocabulary

das Land	die Nationalität	die Sprache
Frankreich	{ der Franzose { die Französin	Französisch

England	{ der Engländer / die Engländerin	Englisch
Schottland	Schotte, Schottin	Schottisch
Irland	Ire, Irin	Irisch
Deutschland	{ der Deutsche / die Deutsche	Deutsch
Österreich	Österreicher, -in	
Italien	Italiener, -in	Italienisch
Spanien	Spanier, -in	Spanisch
die Vereinigten Staaten	Amerikaner, -in	
die Schweiz	Schweizer, -in	
Holland	Holländer, -in	Holländisch
Belgien	Belgier, -in	Flämisch
Schweden	Schwede, Schwedin	Schwedisch
Rußland	Russe, Russin	Russisch
die Tschechoslowakei	Tscheche, Tschechin	Tschechisch
Nordamerika	Nordamerikaner, -in	
Südafrika	Südafrikaner, -in	
die Türkei	Türke, Türkin	Türkisch

in England, in England	die Frau, lady, woman
nach England, to England	der Völkerbund, League of Nations
in Berlin, in Berlin	
nach Berlin, to Berlin	Genf, Geneva
aus Moskau, from Moscow	in der Schweiz, in Switzerland
der Bolschewist, Bolshevik	in die Schweiz, to Switzerland
der Faschist, Fascist	der Gesandte, ambassador
der Herr, gentleman	

Exercise 24

Der Gesandte aus Berlin ist jetzt in London. Ich schickte meinen Bruder nach Genf. Es sind keine Äpfel in dem Garten. Unser Haus ist in dieser Straße. Ein Spanier aus Madrid ist unten. Hast du meine Handschuhe? Er ist der Neffe eines Lehrers in Köln (Cologne). Wo ist deine Uhr? Hier ist sie. Ottos Anzug war in diesem Zimmer. Ist dies Ihr Hut? Wo ist Marie? Ist dies nicht Ihre Armbanduhr (wrist-watch)? Der Neffe dieser Frau ist tot. Ich reiche meinem Onkel seinen Hut. Unsere Kühe sind auf dem Feld. Marie Schmidts (Smith's) Onkel ist in Paris, und Wilhelms Vater ist in der Schweiz. Die Schwester von Fritz ist in dem Laden ihres Onkels.

Exercise 25

Did he not send any (= sent he no) stockings with the shoes? Her dresses are always very good. I often send (= send often) apples and nuts from my garden to my nephews in Germany. We sometimes visit (= visit sometimes) our uncle in Switzerland. Did you send your nephew to Geneva or to Rome (Rom)? Max's shoes are black and Gisela's gloves are brown. Where is your uncle's house? It is in London. Are the rooms of his house very big? He did not send any (= sent no) buttons with her dresses. Have you a Paris newspaper? My uncle hasn't a car. Did you send my brother's books to London? The houses of our city are tall and beautiful.

LESSON VIII

RULES FOR GENDER

In a general way, every noun meaning a male person or animal is masculine, and every noun meaning a female person or animal is feminine. But the endings of words have so much to do with gender that we cannot depend entirely upon the meaning. In what follows we must try to learn something about the *meanings* of endings, as well as their power in determining gender.

Feminine Terminations

1. In English our great feminine ending is *-ess*: actor, actress, etc. In German the corresponding termination is -in: Spieler = a player, Spielerin = a female player. These nouns double the n before adding -en for the plural: thus, the plural of Königin (queen) is Königinnen.

2. Most abstract nouns in German are feminine: that is, nouns denoting qualities or abstractions, such as—

truth (Wahrheit), science (Wissenschaft), beauty (Schön-heit), gratitude (Dankbarkeit), slavery (Sklaverei'), rescue (Rettung), music (Musik'), harmony (Harmonie'). You will observe that all these nouns are derived from simpler words. Wahr means *true*, Wahrheit, the quality of being true; wissen means *to know*, Wissenschaft, the quality of knowing. These words are therefore called derivative words. The most common terminations which are used to form feminine derivative nouns are: -ung (Eng. *-ing*), -heit (Eng. *-hood*), -schaft (Eng. *-ship*), -ei (Eng. *-y*), and -keit (for which we have no English equivalent).

3. The third rule for feminines is of the greatest possible use. All two-syllabled nouns ending in -e, and meaning things without life, are feminine: as die Tasche = the pocket. This rule has few exceptions.

4. The fourth rule is not so important. Most nouns derived from verbs and ending in -d and -t are feminine. Thus: jagen (to hunt) gives die Jagd (the hunting); fahren (to travel) gives die Fahrt (the journey).

Neuter Terminations

1. -chen and -lein are two terminations which make what are called diminutives of the nouns they are attached to. Bach = a brook, Bächlein = little brook *or* brooklet; Dorf = a village, Dörfchen = a little village. -chen and -lein also express endearment, as Väterchen, Mütterchen. These endings make the noun neuter, whatever its gender was before: thus Fräulein, which means a young or unmarried lady (little Frau), is neuter. Note also that where possible the vowel of the noun is always modified.

2. The -en of the Infinitive must be regarded as a neuter termination when the Infinitive is used as a noun. Thus: das Jagen = hunting, das Trinken = drinking.

Masculine Terminations

1. Most nouns ending in -en (excluding Infinitives and diminutives) are masculine.

2. Two-syllabled nouns ending in -ich, -ig and -ing are masculine.

So far as is consistent with the above rules the following considerations of *meaning* may be applied in determining gender.

Masculine are names of days, months, seasons, stones, winds.

Neuter are names of metals (except der Stahl, steel), countries, cities, villages, islands.

Exercise 26

Keeping in view all that has been said, arrange the following nouns into three classes according as they are masculine, feminine or neuter. Go down the columns, not across the page.

Fürstin, princess
Eiche, oak
Honig, honey
Leben, living
Eselei, stupid conduct
Teppich, carpet
Februar, February
Gold, gold
Übersetzung, translation
Schlacht, battle
Garten, garden
Griechenland, Greece
Stunde, hour
Jüngling, youngster
Reinheit, purity
Paris, Paris
Freundschaft, friendship
Diamant', diamond
Schrift, writing
Poesie', poetry
Rauchen, smoking
Freitag, Friday
Frau, wife

Blume, flower
Kindlein, baby
Treppe, staircase
Regen, rain
Edelstein, precious stone
Fröhlichkeit, joyfulness
Büchlein, little book
Melodie', melody
Eisen, iron
Löwe, lion
Sonne, sun
Liebling, darling
Väterchen, little father
Dummheit, stupidity
Helgoland, Heligoland
Käfig, cage
Tanzen, dancing
Monat, month
Pferdchen, little horse
Kuchen, cake
Union, union
Blümchen, little flower

LESSON IX

NON-PERSONAL ELEMENT IN VERBS

Not every part of a verb has person. We can say *I* did it, or *you* did it, or *they* did it. But we cannot use any of these pronouns with *done*. We cannot say I *done* it, or you *done* it, or they *done* it. It is true we can say I (or you or they) *have* done it. But here the personal pronouns do not belong to the *done* but to the *have*. In other words, *have* is a personal part of the verb; *done* is a non-personal. *Done* is called the Past Principle, and can never be used with a personal pronoun without the help of another verb like *have* or *was*. It is for this reason that certain verbs—such as *to have* and *to be*—are called auxiliary or helping verbs.

In English the most common ending for the Past Participle is *-ed*—he has play-ed, work-ed, arrang-ed, borrow-ed, etc. Here are some examples of English and German Past Participles:

Present Tense	loves	liebt	plays	spielt	says sagt
Past Tense	loved	liebte	played	spielte	said sagte
Past Participle	loved	geliebt	played	gespielt	said gesagt

From this we may infer that most German Past Participles begin with ge and end with t.

Once we know the Past Participle of a verb, we can use it to make a new Past tense by the help of *have*. Thus: er hat gesagt = *he has said*, or simply *he said*. This tense is called the *Perfect*, because the action is now complete. Again we may say, er hatte gesagt = he *had* said. This is called the *Pluperfect* tense, because the action was completed at some time now past.

Perfect of lieben

Singular

1.	ich habe geliebt	I have loved
2.	du hast geliebt	thou hast loved
3.	er hat geliebt	he has loved

Plural

1. wir haben geliebt   we have loved
2. { Sie haben / ihr habt } geliebt   you have loved
3. sie haben geliebt   they have loved

Here we see that geliebt remains unchanged. Everything depends upon the personal verb haben. Geliebt, in fact, is hardly a verb at all: it is really a sort of adjective. The Germans throw the Past Participle always away to the very end of the sentence. We say, *he has said the word*. The Germans say, *he has the word said*: er hat das Wort gesagt. *The child had loved the mother of his friend* = Das Kind hatte die Mutter seines Freundes geliebt.

The Infinitive is another non-personal part of the verb, and is treated in the same unceremonious way by the Germans, who put it at the very end. *I will not say the word* = Ich will das Wort nicht sagen. Observe that *say* is here Infinitive, though the *to* is omitted, just as the zu is omitted before sagen. The full Infinitive in German is zu sagen, but the zu is omitted with auxiliaries, as here. Examples will be given later in the Course of the retention of this zu.

In English all Past Participles do not end in *ed*, though that is the regular ending. The following are Past Participles: *done, been, drunk, slept, arisen*. In the same way all German Past Participles do not begin with ge and end with t, though that is the regular thing. In the following list of verbs the first nine are regular, the last six irregular:

Pres. Infin.	Past Tense	Past Part.	Meaning
kaufen	kaufte	gekauft	to buy
suchen	suchte	gesucht	to seek
töten	tötete	getötet	to kill
warten	wartete	gewartet	to wait
bauen	baute	gebaut	to build
antworten	antwortete	geantwortet	to answer
wählen	wählte	gewählt	to choose
retten	rettete	gerettet	to save

Pres. Infin.	Past Tense	Past Part.	Meaning
arbeiten	arbeitete	gearbeitet	to work
brennen	brannte	gebrannt[1]	to burn
denken	dachte	gedacht	to think
bringen	brachte	gebracht	to bring
senden	sandte	gesandt	to send
nennen	nannte	genannt	to name
kennen	kannte	gekannt	to know[2]

You will observe that when the stem of a regular verb ends in -d or -t, an extra e is inserted in the Past and Past Participle. This is for the sake of the sound; your ear will keep you right in this matter.

The Use of the Perfect

This tense is used to express an action that has been going on and is still continuing, or a finished action of recent occurrence, or vaguely in the past. For example:

Ich habe meine Handschuhe gesucht. I have been looking for my gloves.
Er hat mir nicht geantwortet. He did not answer me.
Der Mönch Schwartz hat das Schießpulver entdeckt. The monk Schwartz discovered gunpowder.

Vocabulary

die See, sea
der Soldat, soldier
das Klavier, piano
die Musik, music
das Radio, wireless, radio
der (Schall)plattenspieler, record-player
der Stuhl, chair
der Teppich, carpet
die Zigarre, cigar
die Zigarette, cigarette
die Pfeife, pipe
der Schnee, snow
die Annonce, advertisement
der Hund, dog
im Winter, in winter
im Sommer, in summer

die Frau, woman, wife
das Land, country
Klavier spielen, to play the piano
Radio hören, to listen to the wireless
gern haben, to like (= have willingly)
gern hören, to like listening (to)
baden, to bathe, swim
gern rauchen, to like smoking
zu Weihnachten, at Christmas
auf, on (top of) (with Dat.)
an, on (side of), to (with Acc.)
der Wald, wood
der Stock, stick

---

[1] When *to burn* means *to burn up* or *consume*, it is verbrennen, verbrannte, verbrannt.

[2] When *to know* means to recognise through the five senses.

Exercise 27

Hast du dem Neffen des Bäckers das Buch des Lehrers geschickt? Ich habe die Löwen in dem Walde gehört. Hat die Magd die Eier nicht gekocht? Mein Bruder hat mit meinem Vater telefoniert. Ich habe meinem Onkel seinen Stock gereicht. Dieses Mädchen hat Klavier gespielt. Rauchen Sie gerne (or gern) Zigaretten? Nein, ich rauche immer eine Pfeife. Zu Weihnachten schicken wir unserem Bruder Äpfel, Nüsse, Bücher und Zigaretten. Hören Sie gern Musik im Radio? Wir haben in einem Hause in diesem Dorf gewohnt. Die Soldaten haben die Hauptstadt des Landes verbrannt. Meine Schwester hat die Annonce in der Zeitung gesucht. Wir haben unseren Hund Mops genannt. Welches Buch hat deine Schwester gewählt? Die Soldaten haben keine Frauen und Kinder getötet. Im Sommer haben wir oft in der See gebadet. Die Schüler haben im Winter mit dem Schnee gespielt. Ich habe Hunde nicht gern.

Exercise 28

Have you (du) been dreaming? No, I have been drawing that house. Which book is on your chair? This carpet is very old. I like listening to the wireless. Does your father like smoking? Yes, he has always smoked cigars. I often smoke (= smoke often) cigars at Christmas. In the summer we have (= have we) visited our uncle in Switzerland. Have you sent the newspapers to Geneva? The baker and his wife have named their child Margarete. The tailor has not made the dress. Otto's sister has been playing the piano, and my brothers have been listening to the music on the wireless. Has the tailor brought the dress? In which shop did you buy (Perfect tense) that hat? Do you like bathing in the sea? I like listening to the record-player.

LESSON X

PERSONAL PRONOUNS

He, she and *it* are easily used in English. But in German they require careful watching. We must not think of sex at all, but only of the gender of the noun to which these little words apply. Talking of the town in German, we must not say it *is fine*, but she *is fine*, since Stadt is feminine: sie ist schön. So of a table we must say he *is round*: er ist rund. Of a girl (Mädchen) we say it *is clever*: es ist geschickt; but we may also say sie ist geschickt. You must therefore never use *he* or *she* or *it* without looking carefully at the gender of the noun referred to.

In English we have these words declined:

	Singular			Plural
	Masc.	Fem.	Neut.	All Genders
Nom.	he	she	it	they
Acc.	him	her	it	them

Corresponding to these we have the German forms:

	Singular		Plural
	Masc.	Fem.	Masc. and Fem.
Nom.	er	sie	sie
Acc.	ihn	sie	sie
Dat.	ihm	ihr	ihnen

I saw him, but not her. Ich sah ihn, aber nicht sie.
I have this book from him. Ich habe dieses Buch von ihm.
We have sent her a present. Wir haben ihr ein Geschenk gesandt.

Pay careful attention to what we have said about *it*. The fact is that the English *it* can be put into German in three different ways according to what *it* refers to. If *it* refers to a table (Tisch), it is masculine and is rendered er; if *it* refers to a street (Straße), it is feminine and is represented by sie; if *it* refers to a book (Buch), it is neuter and is rendered by es. All these are Nominative: if *it* is in the Accusative, it is ihn (m.), or sie (f.), or es (n.). You will learn the use of these words much better from observing the following examples:

> Where is my pen? I saw it in your room. Wo ist meine Feder? Ich sah sie in Ihrem Zimmer.
> She has brought my shoe: where is it? Sie hat meinen Schuh gebracht: wo ist er?
> Where is the dog? We have sent it to him. Wo ist der Hund? Wir haben ihn ihm gesandt.
> It was my house, but the soldiers have burned it. Es war mein Haus, aber die Soldaten haben es verbrannt.

The *pronoun as an object*, whether direct (Accusative) or indirect (Dative), *precedes a noun object*, *i.e.* it follows the verb. *Of two pronoun objects*, the *direct* (Accusative) *precedes the indirect* (Dative), that is, the opposite order to two noun objects. *E.g.*:

> Ich schicke es dem Bäcker. I send it to the baker.
> Ich schicke es ihm. I send it to him.

Vocabulary

der Baum, tree	hell, bright
der Wind, wind	stark, strong
die Sonne, sun	schwach, weak
der Mond, moon	teuer, dear
der Stern, star	billig, cheap
der Rasen, lawn	heiß, hot
das Wetter, weather	warm, warm
die Wolke, cloud	kalt, cold
der Regen, rain	jung, young
der Teich, pond	wer? who?
der Nebel, fog	wen? whom? (Acc.)
der Fluß, river	wem? to whom? (Dat.)
das Wasser, water	wann? when?
kaum, scarcely	niemals, never
nur, only	nichts, nothing
gestern, yesterday	schon, already

Exercise 29

Ich habe nichts gehört. Gestern war die Sonne sehr warm. Wem hast du den Weihnachtsbaum (Christmas-) geschickt? Ich habe ihn meinem Neffen geschickt.

Die Wolken sind groß und schwarz, sie bringen Regen. Das Wetter ist sehr kalt, und es (= there) ist Nebel auf dem Fluß. Wann haben Sie diesen Anzug gekauft? Ich habe ihn gestern in dem Laden gekauft. War er billig oder teuer? Er war sehr billig. Die Sterne sind klein, aber der Mond ist groß. Haben Sie Ihrer Schwester die Armbanduhr geschickt? Ja, ich habe sie ihr gestern geschickt. Hat dein Vater den Kindern den Weihnachtsbaum geschickt? Ja, er hat ihn ihnen gestern geschickt. Es sind drei Hunde auf dem Rasen; mein Neffe spielt mit ihnen.

Exercise 30

The sun was not very bright yesterday. When did you answer? There were seven or eight sailors on the river. This river is very long. We scarcely heard (= heard scarcely) the children's song. Whom did you visit in Switzerland? These motor-cars are almost too cheap. Whom did you telephone yesterday? Here is your hat. Where did you buy it? I am sending it (*i.e.* the hat) to my brother. The children have been looking for the apples. I have handed them to them. We never have (= have never) fog in this country. Who answered him? Have you 'phoned her? Was the wind very strong yesterday? The sky was blue and the clouds were small and white. The water in the pond was too cold yesterday. We did not bathe. I have said nothing to him. She only smiled (= smiled only). We scarcely heard them.

LESSON XI

STRONG VERBS

Taking the three parts of the verb—the Infinitive, the Imperfect, and the Past Participle—we find that most of the verbs with which we have dealt up till now have had the form lieben, liebte, geliebt; spielen, spielte, gespielt. This is what is known as the *Weak* Conjugation, or the *New* Conjugation. The best way to learn the difference between the New and the Old Conjugation is to examine the following list of verbs, and see how they differ from the verbs we have been dealing with:

Some Verbs of the Strong or Old Conjugation

Infinitive	Imperfect	Past Part.	Meaning
schlagen	schlug	geschlagen	to strike
geben	gab	gegeben	to give
heißen	hieß	geheißen	to be called
nehmen	nahm	genommen	to take
reiten	ritt	geritten	to ride
laufen	lief	gelaufen	to run
kommen	kam	gekommen	to come
singen	sang	gesungen	to sing
essen	aß	gegessen	to eat (of people)
fressen	fraß	gefressen	to eat (of animals)
spinnen	spann	gesponnen	to spin
trinken	trank	getrunken	to drink
fliegen	flog	geflogen	to fly
sehen	sah	gesehen	to see
stehen	stand	gestanden	to stand
brechen	brach	gebrochen	to break
beginnen	begann	begonnen	to begin
sprechen	sprach	gesprochen	to speak
fahren	fuhr	gefahren	to drive

Read over the above list five or six times, so as to impress the general run of the sound upon the ear.

On careful examination, you will note several points in which all those verbs agree with each other, and differ from the lieben, liebte, geliebt conjugation.

1. The Past Participles *all end in* -en, not in t.

2. The Imperfect has *no ending at all,* instead of -te.

3. The *vowel of the Imperfect is always different* from the vowel of the Infinitive.

You will note that some of the verbs have three different vowel sounds, others have only two. When there are only two sounds, sometimes it is the Infinitive and sometimes the Imperfect which is the same as the Past Participle.

As a test at this stage, arrange the above nineteen verbs in three classes: (1) Those having three different vowel sounds; (2) those in which the Infinitive and Past Participle have the same vowel; and (3) those in which the Imperfect and the Past Participle have the same vowel.

Observe now the full conjugation of the Imperfect, and note how it differs from the liebte type:

Imperfect of Certain Strong or Old Verbs

1.	ich	schlug	lief	aß	sah	kam
2.	du	schlugst	liefst	aßest	sahst	kamst
3.	er	schlug	lief	aß	sah	kam
1.	wir	schlugen	liefen	aßen	sahen	kamen
2. {	Sie	schlugen	liefen	aßen	sahen	kamen
	ihr	schlugt	lieft	aßt	saht	kamt
3.	sie	schlugen	liefen	aßen	sahen	kamen

Clearly the most striking difference is *the total absence of any termination in both first and third person singular.* You cannot help noting how exceedingly regular the conjugation is. Given the first person singular you cannot fail to complete the whole.

With the Present tense of old or strong verbs this regularity is not present. The plural of the Present tense is all right: it is, indeed, simply the Infinitive with the usual pronouns placed before it. Even in the singular the first person always has the same vowel as the Infinitive. It is the second and third persons singular that give trouble by sometimes changing their vowel sounds. You will understand this better by examining carefully the following:

Present of Certain Strong or Old Verbs

1. ich	schlage	laufe	esse	sehe	komme
2. du	schlägst	läufst	ißt	siehst	kommst
3. er	schlägt	läuft	ißt	sieht	kommt
1. wir	schlagen	laufen	essen	sehen	kommen
2. { Sie	schlagen	laufen	essen	sehen	kommen
{ ihr	schlagt	lauft	eßt	seht	kommt
3. sie	schlagen	laufen	essen	sehen	kommen

The change of vowel in the 2nd and 3rd person does not always take place, as we find from kommen, although the verb stoßen, *to push*, has du stöß(es)t, er stößt. The main changes are:

(i) a is changed into ä
(ii) au ,, ,, äu
(iii) e (long) is changed into ie
(iv) e (short) ,, ,, i

Keeping in view all that has been said, write out, as above, the Present and the Imperfect of the following six verbs:

bitten	bat	gebeten	to beg *or* ask
befehlen	befahl	befohlen	to command
sterben	starb	gestorben	to die
fahren	fuhr	gefahren	to drive
geben	gab	gegeben	to give
nehmen	nahm	genommen	to take

Notice that geben (although e long) has gibst, gibt, and nehmen has nimmst, nimmt in the Present tense. The form giebst, giebt is old-fashioned.

[See Appendix B, pp. 188–192.]

Vocabulary

das Pferd, horse	das Heu, hay
der Esel, donkey	das Gras, grass
die Katze, cat	der Tee, tea
das Schwein, pig	der Zucker, sugar

die Biene, bee
die Wespe, wasp
die Spinne, spider
der Feldarbeiter, farm-hand
der Bauernhof, farm
der Bauer, farmer
die Bäuerin, farmer's wife
der Stall, stable
die Peitsche, whip
das Brot, bread
der Honig, honey
die Arbeit, work
von . . . zu, from . . . to
laut, loud, loudly

die Blume, flower
das Gewebe, web
melken, to milk
füttern, to feed
pflügen, to plough
säen, to sow
bellen, to bark
miauen, to mew
summen, to buzz
iahen, to bray
grunzen, to grunt
im Frühling, in spring
im Herbst, in the autumn
was? what?

Exercise 31

Die Spinne war groß und dick; sie spann ein Gewebe.
Die Biene summte; sie flog von Blume zu Blume und
suchte Honig. Was frißt die Wespe? Sie frißt Zucker.
Die Esel iahten, die Schweine grunzten, die Hunde
bellten, und die Katzen miauten. Der Feldarbeiter ritt
auf einem Pferd. Er fütterte die Ochsen, die Schafe und
die Kühe. Sein Hund lief mit ihm. Er bellte zu laut.
Der Bauer schlug ihn mit seiner Peitsche. Die Bäuerin
melkte (or molk) die Kühe in dem Stall. Es sind acht
oder neun Feldarbeiter auf dem Bauernhof. Sie arbeiten
immer. Im Herbst pflügen sie die Felder. Im Frühling
säen sie. Der Bauer hieß Herr Braun. Er stand auf
(got up) und begann seine Arbeit. Er fuhr in seinem
Wagen zu dem Feld. Was aß er? Er aß Brot und
trank Tee mit Zucker. Seine Kinder sangen Lieder.
Er gab ihnen Äpfel und Nüsse.

Exercise 32

The farmer drove to the fields. He took his children
(add *with*, him being understood). They liked to see
(= saw willingly) the cows, sheep and horses in the fields.
The boy was called Karl. He liked to ride on a donkey.
He gave it (= him) hay. The donkey likes eating sugar.

Karl's dog is in the garden. It is big and strong. It
breaks the flowers. Karl runs after him and strikes him

with his whip. The dog barks loudly. The sun is warm and bright. The bees are buzzing and flying from flower to flower. They like honey. Do you like honey? Karl does not see the spider. It is big and fat. It has spun a web. Do you like spiders?

Have you already begun your work? I have broken[1] my watch. Has your uncle given his nephew a watch? Have you (du) drunk your tea? Yes, and I have already eaten my bread and honey.

LESSON XII

PREPOSITIONS AND WERDEN

With Accusative or Dative

We have had some prepositions that govern the dative and some that govern the accusative. But now we must have some that sometimes govern the dative and sometimes the accusative. There are nine of them:

an, at (with dat.)
an, to (with acc.)
auf, on, upon
hinter, behind
in, in or at (with dat.)
in, into (with acc.)

neben, beside, near
über, over or across
vor, before, in front of
unter, under or among
zwischen, between

The meaning tells us when to use the accusative, when the dative. If there is any *motion towards* anything implied, then the accusative is used; if no such motion is implied, the dative.

Er ist auf dem Berge.	He is on the mountain.
Er läuft auf dem Berge.	He runs on the mountain.
Er läuft auf den Berg.	He runs to the mountain.
Er ging in das Haus.	He went into the house.
Er war in dem Hause.	He was in the house.
Sie saß auf dem Stuhl.	She sat on the chair.
Sie sprang auf den Stuhl.	She jumped on to the chair.

---

[1] Use zerbrechen.

With Dative only

To keep matters clear we had better repeat the more common prepositions that govern only the dative:

aus, out of	samt ⎫
bei, by, at, with, near	nebst ⎬ along with
gegenüber, opposite	seit, since
mit, with	von, of, from, by
nach, after, to	zu, to, at

Gegenüber often follows the noun.

With Accusative only

durch, through	ohne, without
für, for	um, about, round
gegen, against	wider, against

With Genitive only

anstatt *or* statt, instead of	trotz, in spite of
diesseits, on this side of	während, during
jenseits, on that side of	wegen, on account of
mittels, by means of	

Observe that all except während have the English equivalent ending in *of*. This is a good way of remembering which case these prepositions govern.

Contraction of Preposition and Article

Just as we contract *do not* into *don't*, so the Germans are fond of contracting their prepositions and their articles into one word. Thus:

an dem	becomes	am	bei dem	becomes	beim
an das	,,	ans	von dem	,,	vom
auf das	,,	aufs	(vor das	,,	vors)
in dem	,,	im	zu dem	,,	zum
in das	,,	ins	zu der	,,	zur

Special Notes on the Translation of *To*

(i) When *to* shows the receiver of an object, use the dative without preposition (see also Lesson XXIV):

Er gab seiner Schwester das Buch.   He gave the book to his sister.

Er schickte Resi ein Buch.   He sent a book to Resi.

(ii) Indicating motion towards a person, zu:

> Er kam zu seiner Mutter.   He came to his mother.

(iii) Motion towards a large object or place (not a proper name), zu:

> Er lief zu dem Bauernhof.   He ran to the farm.
> N.B.   From . . . to = von . . . zu.

(iv) Motion towards smaller objects, and sending letters to persons, an:

> Er ging an das Fenster (an den Spiegel, an die Tür).   He went to the window (mirror, door).
> Ich schrieb einen Brief an meine Mutter.   I wrote a letter to my mother.

—although one would not usually use an with a pronoun in this case, but the dative of the pronoun:

> Ich schrieb ihr einen Brief.

(v) *To* before a place (proper name), nach:

> Wir fuhren nach Spanien, nach Köln.   We went to Spain, to Cologne.

(vi) *To* = auf in the following cases:

> Auf die Post, auf den Markt, auf die Universität, auf die Polizei, auf die Bank, to the post-office (the market, university, police-station, bank).
> N.B.   To (into) the country, auf das Land.   To the seaside, an die See.

(vii) When *into* as well as *to* is implied, in:

> Er geht in die Schule, in die Kirche, in die Stadt, ins Kino, ins Theater.   He is going to school, to church, to the town, cinema, theatre.

(viii) To talk *to*, sprechen mit:

> Ich sprach mit dem Bürgermeister.   I was talking to the mayor.

(ix) *To* = in order to, um . . . zu (+ Infinitive):

> Er ging aus, um die Pferde zu füttern.   He went out to feed the horses.

(x) Note the following indefinite directions:

Nach rechts (links), to the right, to the left.
Von oben nach unten, from top to bottom.
Von hinten nach vorn, from back to front.

Vocabulary

die Tür, door
das Tor, gate
die Mauer, wall[1]
das Restaurant, restaurant
der Park (—s, —s),[2] park
der Fußgänger, pedestrian
das Warenhaus, big stores
die Straße, street
die Straßenlampe, street-lamp
der Brief, letter
der Polizist, policeman
die Straßenecke, street-corner
die Brücke, bridge
das Rathaus, Town Hall
das Schaufenster, shop-window
der Marktplatz, market-place
der Briefkasten, letter-box
das Gebäude, building
*schließen, to shut
angestellt, employed

das Café (—s, —s),[2] café
beim Lebensmittelhändler, at the grocer's
das Krankenhaus, hospital
der Verkehr, traffic
die Telefonzelle, telephone-box
der Wolkenkratzer, skyscraper
*liegen, to lie, be situated
kaufen, to buy
verkaufen, to sell
prachtvoll, magnificent
gefährlich, dangerous
führen, to lead, drive, take
*wiegen, to weigh
verlangen, to ask for, demand
bewundern, to admire
bezahlen, to pay (for)
nach Hause *gehen, to go home
zu Hause *sein, to be at home

* From now on strong verbs are marked with an asterisk (*), and their principal parts are to be found in the Appendix, pp. 188–192.

A Note on the English *to put*

Some care must be exercised in translating *to put*. Note the following:

   (i) In a general way, setzen.
   (ii) To put a thing *standing up* (as a vase), stellen.
   (iii) To put a thing *lying down* (as a book), legen.
   (iv) To put away out of sight, as in a drawer, pocket, etc., stecken.
   (v) To put = to add (as salt in potatoes, etc.), *tun (literally *to do*).

---

[1] die Wand is the surface, die Mauer the thickness.
[2] Gen, sing. and Nom. pl.

Exercise 33

Unsere Bank liegt zwischen der Post und der Marien-kirche.[1] Ich habe mit meinem Bruder aus einer Telefon-zelle telefoniert. Es sind viele Wolkenkratzer in unserer Stadt. Das Gebäude des Völkerbundes war in Genf, in der Schweiz. Es waren Bolschewisten in Rußland und Faschisten in Italien und Deutschland. Die Soldaten sind vor dem Tore der Stadt. Es sind Italiener und Spanier.

Ich ging ins Restaurant. Ich habe gegessen und bezahlt. Ich kam aus dem Restaurant und ging zum Marktplatz. Ich ging ins Kino. Das Kino war groß und schön, aber es war kein Wolkenkratzer. Im Kino waren Männer, Frauen und Kinder. Ich gehe oft ins Theater. Gehen Sie gern ins Theater? Ich sah ein Krankenhaus neben dem Park. Gegenüber dem Waren-haus (Dem Warenhaus gegenüber) war das Rathaus. Dieses Gebäude ist prachtvoll. Ich sagte zu einem Polizisten: "Wo ist ein Briefkasten?" Er antwortete: "Dort an der Straßenecke." Ich steckte einen Brief in den Briefkasten. Mein Bruder ist bei einem Lebens-mittelhändler angestellt. Er verkauft Zucker, Tee usw.[2] Hinter dem Rathaus war die Paulskirche.[3] Ich ging unter eine Brücke. Diese Brücke war sehr hoch. Über die Brücke fahren Autos und Autobusse (buses). Der Verkehr ist sehr gefährlich für die Fußgänger

Exercise 34

I put my book on a chair. The weather was fairly warm. I ran out of the room. I went through the door and into[4] the street. It was dark but the street was fairly bright on account of (because of, owing to) the street-lamps. There were eight motor-cars and three

---

[1] die Marienkirche, St. Mary's Church.
[2] usw. = und so weiter, and so on, *or* etc.
[3] die Paulskirche, St. Paul's Church.
[4] Of persons, vehicles, etc. *auf*, otherwise *in* before *Straße*

horses in the street. I went with my dog round the town. My dog ran between the motor-cars. I went into a telephone box and 'phoned my sister. She is employed in a hospital near St. Paul's Church. I live with my brother opposite the Town Hall. We went to the right and came to a bridge. It was fairly low. We looked down[1] on to the traffic. The traffic since the war is very dangerous. My uncle was in that car. He was driving to the market-place. He has a shop there. He often drives (= drives often) over this bridge. Our village lay on the other side of the river. In front of our house stood a lamp-post (street-lamp). We went into a restaurant to eat. After the meal[2] I went home without my dog, but I saw him at home, in front of the door.

There is a very useful little verb called werden, which means to *become* or to *get*, in the sense of *getting* angry or *getting* grey. The Present Indicative goes quite easily:

Present of werden

Singular	Plural
1. ich werde	wir werden
2. du wirst	{ Sie werden { ihr werdet
3. er wird	sie werden

The great use of this verb is to form the Future of all other verbs. To make the Future all we have to do is to add the Infinitive of the verb we want to the proper part of werden:

I shall buy.	Ich werde kaufen.
You will speak.	Sie werden sprechen.
The boy will learn.	Der Knabe wird lernen.
The horse will run.	Das Pferd wird laufen.

If we want to have what is called the *Future Perfect*— *i.e.* to express something that will be completely done at some future time—we have to use haben along with the Past Participle of the required verb:

[1] To look down on, sehen auf (*acc.*).
[2] The meal, das Essen.

I shall have bought.	Ich werde gekauft haben.
You will have spoken.	Sie werden gesprochen haben.
The boy will have learnt.	Der Knabe wird gelernt haben.

The Perfect tense of haben is formed in the ordinary way:

> Ich habe viele Äpfel von diesem Baum gehabt.   I have had many apples from this tree.

But the Perfect tense of sein is formed with the Present tense of sein + Past Participle:

> ich bin gewesen, I have been (*literally*: I am been).
> du bist gewesen, you have been.
> er ist gewesen, he has been, etc.

Vocabulary

morgen, tomorrow
morgen früh, tomorrow morning
nächste Woche, next week
nächsten Sonntag, next Sunday
  ,,   Montag, ,, Monday
  ,,   Dienstag, ,, Tuesday
  ,,   Mittwoch, ,, Wednesday
  ,,   Donnerstag, next Thursday
  ,,   Freitag, next Friday
  ,,   Samstag, ,, Saturday
heute, today
heute morgen, this morning
heute nachmittag, this afternoon
heute abend, this evening
der Freund, friend
das Flugzeug, aeroplane
um zwei Uhr, at 2 o'clock
um halb vier, at half past three

am Abend, in the evening
am Nachmittag, in the afternoon
abends, in the evening(s)
morgens, in the morning(s)
nachmittags, in the afternoon(s)
bald, soon
früh, early
letzt, last
spät, late
schnell, quickly
eines Tages, one day
nächstes Jahr, next year
der Bahnhof, station (railway)
die U-bahn (die Untergrundbahn), Underground (railway), tube
*bekommen, to get, receive

Exercise 35

Morgen werde ich zum Marktplatz gehen. Was werden Sie dort tun? Ich werde zwei oder drei Pferde kaufen. Sind sie billig oder teuer? Sie sind dieses Jahr ziemlich teuer. Werden Sie mit[1] dem Auto fahren?

[1] To travel *by* a car or train, fahren mit; *by* aeroplane, fliegen mit.

Heute ist das Wetter sehr kalt.   Wir werden bald Schnee haben.   Was wird dein Onkel nächsten Dienstag tun? Er wird nach Lissabon[1] fliegen.   Heute nachmittag werden wir ins Kino gehen.   Gehen Sie gern ins Kino? Meine Brüder werden eines Tages nach Köln fliegen. Heute abend wird meine Schwester Klavier spielen, und Elses Bruder wird Lieder singen.   Ich werde die Musik im Radio hören.   Ich höre gerne Radio.

Gestern habe ich einen Brief von meinem Onkel bekommen. Zu Weihnachten wird er meinem Vater einen Weihnachtsbaum schicken.   Er ist letzte Woche in Frankreich gewesen.   Das Wetter war sehr kalt dort.   Sie haben Nebel und Regen gehabt.   Ich bin niemals in Frankreich gewesen.   Warst du schon in Paris?[2]

Exercise 36

Next Friday I shall travel to Germany.   Will you go by car to London?   No, I shall travel by the Underground (by tube).   What will you do in Germany? I shall visit one or two friends.   Will you go (= fly) by air (= with the aeroplane)?   No, I don't like travelling by air.   Have you ever been to Germany?[2]   Yes, I was there last year (= last year there).   To which station will you go?   To Liverpool Street.[3]   The weather has not been very warm.

[1] Lisbon.
[2] Were you already in = have you ever been to?
[3] Do not translate.

LESSON XIII

DECLENSION OF ADJECTIVES

Words which indicate qualities in connection with nouns and pronouns are called adjectives. We have already used several of them, such as gut, schlecht, böse, arm, jung. But if you care to look back over your exercises you will find that all the adjectives we have used have been used along with some part of the verb *to be*. We have never used an adjective *before* a noun. We have said often something like *the man is good*: we have never spoken of *the good man*.

The first way (the man is good) is called the *predicative* use of the adjective; the second (the good man) is called the *attributive* use of the adjective. In English there is no difference in the form of the word *good*: it is exactly the same in both cases. In German there is a very important difference. In the predicative use the adjective does not change at all. If you look back at all the exercises and examples you will not find any change in any adjective.[1]

But in the attributive use the adjective must be declined so as to agree with its noun in both number and gender. We say, der Mann ist gut; ein Mädchen ist gut; die Stadt ist gut; die Knaben sind gut: using the same word gut in every case. But we must say, ein guter Mann; ein gutes Mädchen; die gute Stadt; die guten Knaben.

The changes that the attributive adjective undergoes are different according to whether an article is or is not used with it. There are three cases:

1. WHEN THE ADJECTIVE IS USED WITHOUT ANY ARTICLE. Here the terminations of the adjective are

[1] We are not speaking here of demonstratives like dieser, or possessives like mein.

merely the terminations of the definite article as they
are changed in the demonstratives like dieser.

| | Singular | | | Plural |
	Masc.	Fem.	Neut.	All Genders
Nom.	-er	-e	-es	-e
Acc.	-en	-e	-es	-e
Gen.	(-es) -en	-er	(-es) -en	-er
Dat.	-em	-er	-em	-en

The -en in the two genitives is put in to show that
now for the sake of sound en is preferred to es. Guten
Brotes seems to sound better than gutes Brotes in the
ears of a German.

2. WHEN THE ADJECTIVE IS USED WITH THE DEFINITE
ARTICLE. Here we have a very pretty form, which is
easily remembered as a mental picture of five e's among
a crowd of en's.

| | Singular | | | Plural |
	Masc.	Fem.	Neut.	All Genders
Nom.	-e	-e	-e	-en
Acc.	-en	-e	-e	-en
Gen.	-en	-en	-en	-en
Dat.	-en	-en	-en	-en

The above form is also used after four words that we
already know: dieser, jener, jeder and welcher, and some
new ones: mancher = many a, derselbe (or der nämliche)
= the same, and der andere = the other.

3. WHEN THE ADJECTIVE IS USED WITH THE INDEFINITE
ARTICLE. This is not quite so regular as No. 2, but *all
the en's remain unchanged*.

| | Singular | | | Plural |
	Masc.	Fem.	Neut.	All Genders
Nom.	-er	-e	-es	-en
Acc.	-en	-e	-es	-en
Gen.	-en	-en	-en	-en
Dat.	-en	-en	-en	-en

The same form is used with the words: mein, dein,
sein, kein, ihr, Ihr, euer, unser.

Notice that after any of the determinative words mentioned (der, mein, kein, welcher, etc.) there is *always* -en *in the Genitive and Dative and always in the Plural*, and if the determinative word ends in -en, then the adjective also ends in -en (masculine singular accusative).

Vocabulary

lustig, jolly, merry
traurig, sad
hübsch, pretty
häßlich, ugly
rein, clean
schmutzig, dirty
klug, clever, intelligent
dumm, silly, stupid
blind, blind
taub, deaf
bequem, comfortable
hart, hard
weich, soft

unbequem, uncomfortable
eng, narrow
breit, broad
stumm, dumb
der Großvater, grandfather
die Großmutter, grandmother
der Vetter (—s, —n), (boy) cousin
die Kusine, (girl) cousin
die Tante, aunt
das Taschentuch, handkerchief
*tragen, to wear, carry

Exercise 37

Give the Nominative Singular, Genitive Singular and Nominative Plural of the following:

einem großen Baum, einer kleinen Blume, keinem blinden Manne, einem kleinen Mädchen, welcher breiten Straße, den starken Hunden, der klugen Kusine, dem tauben Vetter, den häßlichen alten Frauen, kaltem Winde, demselben schmutzigen Jungen.

Exercise 38

Das traurige Mädchen weint immer. Deutsche Bücher sind nicht immer schwer. Die kleine Tochter des dicken Bäckers gab dem klugen Neffen des alten Schneiders einen Brief. Ein kluger Junge lernt schnell. Die kleinen Kinder spielten auf dem weichen Gras. Sie spielen nicht gern auf der harten Straße. Der alte Großvater ist blind, und seine alte Frau ist sehr taub.

Das hübsche Mädchen trägt ein neues Kleid mit roten Knöpfen. Karl hat ein reines Taschentuch in der Tasche seines braunen Anzugs. Der Verkehr ist in diesen engen Straßen sehr gefährlich. Zwei blinde Männer gingen mit ihrem weißen Hunde über die breite Straße. Hübsche Mädchen sind nicht immer dumm.

Exercise 39

Little boys are nearly always dirty. I shall visit an old friend in Geneva. Blind men are not always sad. The narrow streets of the old city were very dark. I do not like this uncomfortable old chair. My beautiful cousin sang French, Spanish and German songs. I like listening to good music on the wireless. The Italian ambassador came to London yesterday (= yesterday to London). Marie's cousin was wearing a green dress and a white hat. Which German book have you chosen?

LESSON XIV

RELATIVE PRONOUNS

Certain pronouns, called relative pronouns, both relate to nouns or pronouns previously mentioned in a sentence, and join clauses together. *The knight who sent it is dead.* Here *who* is a relative pronoun, referring back to *knight*, and at the same time joining the clause *the knight is dead* to the clause *who sent it.* Some people say that *who* here is equal to *and he.*

There are two ways of translating the relative pronouns into German.

The shorter and more frequently used form of the German relative is nothing but the definite article with the genitive singular, the genitive and dative plural changed somewhat.

		Singular				Plural All Genders
	Masc.		Fem.	Neut.		
Nom.	der	who	die	das	which *or* that	die
Acc.	den	whom	die	das	which *or* that	die
Gen.	dessen	whose	deren	dessen	of which	deren
Dat.	dem	to whom	der	dem	to which	denen

Note that the dative plural of the relative is denen, to show that it *is* plural. With the article, den is enough, for the noun shows whether it is singular or plural.

		Singular				Plural All Genders
	Masc.		Fem.	Neut.		
Nom.	welcher	who	welche	welches	which	welche
Acc.	welchen	whom	welche	welches	which	welche
Gen.	dessen	whose	deren	dessen	of which	deren
Dat.	welchem	to whom	welcher	welchem	to which	welchen

The resemblance of the above declension to the interrogative welcher is very plain. The genitive is the case that demands your attention.

The English meanings given above apply only to English nouns. If welches refers to a person it must be translated not *which*, but *who*.

> Das Mädchen, das (or welches) die Eier gekauft hat, ist jung. The girl, *who* bought the eggs, is young.
> Die Stadt, die (or welche) er gerettet hatte, war sehr alt. The town, *which* he had saved, was very old.
> Er hat einen Teller gekauft, den (or welchen) er in der Stadt gesehen hatte. He has bought a plate, *which* he had seen in the city.

In all these examples you will observe the peculiar place of the verb in the clause to which the relative belongs. In all these clauses the personal verb is put *at the end*.

> Der Ritter, den Ihre Freunde gestern sahen, ist tot. The knight, whom your friends saw yesterday, is dead.

Observe the punctuation in the examples given: every relative sentence is enclosed between two commas.

In English we could, if we liked, leave out the *whom*,

and say only, *the knight your friends saw yesterday is dead*. But in German this is NEVER allowed. The relative can never be omitted.

The genitive of the relative must always in German come *before* the noun to which it refers. We say in English, *the house the doors of which have fallen*. In German this must run, das Haus, dessen Türen gefallen sind. In other words, we must always use in German *whose* instead of *of which*. *Whose* always comes before its noun in English, and takes away the need of the article: thus, *a coat, of which the sleeve was torn*, should be put into German in the form, *a coat, whose sleeve was torn*. Here the article *the* is got rid of altogether.

When referring to things wo- or wor- followed by a preposition may be used instead of the usual relative pronoun:

> Das Flugzeug, mit dem (or womit) er nach Deutschland flog, verunglückte. The aeroplane in which he was travelling to Germany crashed.

Was is used to translate *which* when referring to a whole clause, and also after the following: alles, everything; vieles, much; nichts, nothing:

> Es rieselte, was dem alten Fischer außerordentlich gefiel. It was drizzling, which pleased the old fisherman immensely.
> Alles, was ich habe, everything I have.
> Nichts, was er sagte, nothing he said.

Vocabulary

der Arzt, doctor
der Metzger, butcher
der Chauffeur, chauffeur
die Stenotypistin, shorthand typist
der Zahn, tooth
der Zahnarzt, dentist
der Jäger, huntsman, hunter
der Dieb, thief, burglar
der Richter, judge
der Briefträger, postman

der Schauspieler, actor
der Filmschauspieler, film actor
der Kaufmann, shopkeeper
der Schriftsteller, author
der Kellner, waiter
*bitten (um), to ask for
*werden, to become
Seemann werden, to become a sailor
Briefträger sein, to be a postman

der Schuhmacher, cobbler	*stehlen, to steal
das Wirtshaus "Zum roten Löwen", Red Lion Inn	heilen, to heal, cure
	*ziehen, to pull, draw
das Wirtshaus "Zur blauen Kuh", Blue Cow Inn	verhaften, to arrest
	reparieren, to mend
der Wirt, landlord, inn-keeper	nach Diktat *schreiben, to take down
der Film, film	
die Rolle, rôle, part	*treffen, to meet
der Kunde, customer	bedienen, to serve
das Kindermädchen, nurse-maid	spazieren *gehen, to go for a walk
der Korb, basket	spazieren führen, to take for a walk
die Schublade, drawer	

Exercise 40

Der Mann, mit dem ich gestern gesprochen habe, ist der Bürgermeister von Brüssel (Brussels). Eine große Filmschauspielerin spielt eine Rolle im Film, den wir heute abend sehen werden. Der Wirt des Wirtshauses "Zum roten Löwen" (der Wirt des "Roten Löwen"), in dem (wo, worin) ich gestern den Chauffeur des Film-schauspielers Willi Fritsch traf, ist Seemann (Matrose) gewesen. Der Schuhmacher, der deine braunen Schuhe repariert hat, ist an der Tür. Der Metzger bediente seine Kunden, unter (= amongst) denen die Frau eines großen Schriftstellers war. Der Korb, in welchem (in dem, worin) sie die Äpfel und Nüsse trug, war ganz neu. Der Zahnarzt, in dessen Haus der Polizist den Dieb verhaftete, hat heute morgen meinen Zahn gezogen. Die Stenotypistin, die diesen Brief nach Diktat schrieb, ist tot.

Exercise 41

You will have seen from the foregoing how important the relative pronoun is, and how considerably it adds to our powers of self-expression. Descriptions which before were detached and awkward now come more naturally.

As an interesting departure from the usual type of exercise the student is asked to rewrite the following pairs of detached sentences, joining each pair by means of a relative pronoun.

We will do one as an example:

(i) Er fuhr das Auto. He was driving the car.
(ii) Das Auto schleuderte auf der nassen Straße. The car skidded on the wet road.
(iii) Das Auto, das er fuhr, schleuderte auf der nassen Straße. The car he was driving skidded on the wet road.

1. Der Briefträger hat einen Brief gebracht. Die Schwester des Briefträgers ist unser Kindermädchen. 2. Der Mann ist der Neffe eines großen Richters. Ich habe mit dem Manne gesprochen. 3. Die Schublade war fast leer. Ich sah den Brief in der Schublade. 4. Die Frau ist sehr reich. Wir sahen gestern ihren Mann in der "Blauen Kuh". 5. Der Kellner bediente den Jäger. Der Jäger ist bei einem sehr reichen Kaufmann angestellt. 6. Der Dieb ist der Bruder eines Polizisten. Der Dieb stahl die Armbanduhr einer großen Filmschauspielerin. 7. Das Kino war groß und prachtvoll. Ich sah diesen Film in dem Kino. 8. Der Arzt ist nach Ägypten (Egypt) gegangen. Der Arzt hat meinen Neffen geheilt. 9. Die Brüder sind im Krankenhaus. Das Flugzeug der Brüder verunglückte.

Exercise 42

The two girls, whose father played a great part in the film "Michael Kohlhaas", were listening to the wireless. The letter which I saw in this drawer was from your brother. The nursemaid who has taken the children for a walk is from Cologne. The doctor whose nephew I met yesterday cured my sister in Switzerland. The house in which he lived had a red roof and a green door. The shorthand typist who took this letter down has a brother who is employed at your uncle's. The man to whom I was speaking yesterday is the landlord of the "Jolly Farmer". The café in which we met him is near the post-office. Everything we saw was white. The postman has a letter which comes from Russia. At the station we saw (= saw we) the brothers who flew last year to America. The waiter whose brothers stole the actress's car was serving the policeman who arrested them. Nothing he does is very good. The weather was bright and warm, which made our work easy.

LESSON XV

ORDER OF WORDS

I. Verb before Subject

If a clause in German begins with an adverb, or an adverbial phrase, the verb and the subject in that clause change places. *Yesterday he was ill* becomes gestern war er krank.

Certain adverbial conjunctions have the power to cause the same change—*inversion* it is usually called—in the clauses they introduce. Some of the most common of these are:

also, so, therefore	jetzt *or* nun, now
auch, also, too	kaum, scarcely
dann, da, then	so, so (= thus)
doch, yet, however	vielmehr, rather
Now he was poor.	Nun war er arm.
Yet she killed her friend.	Doch tötete sie ihren Freund.

We are not to think this is a remarkable thing in German. In English we cannot say: *Scarcely he was dead*; the order must be as in German: Kaum war er tot.

2. Verb at End of Clause

In German, however, this system of changed order is carried further. For all conjunctions which introduce dependent clauses have the peculiar effect of throwing the personal verb in the dependent clause to the very end of that clause.

Some of the commonest of such subordinating conjunctions are:

als, as, when (past time)	daß, that
wenn, when (pres. or fut.)	bis, until
wenn, whenever	sobald, as soon as
wenn, if	obgleich, although
ob, if, whether	weil, because
wie, as, how	indem, whilst
da, as, since	bevor, before
während, whilst	so daß, so that

Er weiß, daß die Kinder böse waren. He knows that the children were wicked.

Die Mutter war krank, weil ihr Sohn sie sehr schlecht behandelte. The mother was ill because her son treated her very badly.

Do not forget the comma! This is most important.

Subordinate Clause + Main Clause

A subordinate clause may precede a main clause, whereas a co-ordinate one (*i.e.* with a conjunction which does not change the word order, like und, *and*, aber, *but*, denn, *for*, oder, *or*) cannot do so, and when this happens the first rule is applied, namely, when the subject does not begin the sentence the verb precedes the subject:

Als er nach Hause kam, sah er seinen Onkel. When he came home he saw his uncle.

Vocabulary

der Fischer, fisherman	bauen, to build
der Fisch, fish	krank, ill
das Boot, boat[1]	die Erkältung, cold (illness)
der See (—s, —n), lake	*fangen, to catch
der Sekretär, secretary	*finden, to find
ins (or zu) Bett gehen, to go to bed	schneien, to snow
regnen, to rain	die Aufgabe, exercise, lesson
rudern, to row	*schließen, to shut
müde, tired	

---

[1] Pronunciation of Boot is, in phonetic symbols, bo:t (see p. 16).

Exercise 43

Begin each of the following sentences with dann, then, bald, soon, gestern, yesterday, einmal, once, eines Tages, one day, or plötzlich, suddenly:

1. Ein armer Fischer wohnte in diesem Dorfe. 2. Wir trafen die Sekretärin des Schriftstellers am Bahnhof. 3. Die Russen bauten neue Schulen und Universitäten. 4. Der Hund lief aus dem Zimmer. 5. Der Schneider kam nach Hause.

Exercise 44

Join up each of the following pairs of sentences so as to make one good compound sentence, as this example shows:

(i) Meine Schwester spielte Klavier. My sister was playing the piano.
(ii) Ich schrieb einen Brief. I wrote a letter.
(iii) Meine Schwester spielte Klavier, während ich einen Brief schrieb. My sister played the piano while I wrote a letter.

You may find it convenient to use an adverbial conjunction instead of a subordinating one, or you may put your subordinate clause first.

1. Er ging ins Hospital. Er war krank. 2. Ich war nicht dort. Er kam nach Hause. 3. Ich werde den Brief schreiben. Ich komme nach Hause. 4. Ich werde meinen Freund besuchen. Ich gehe ins Kino. 5. Er trägt keinen Mantel. Es ist sehr kalt. 6. Wir hatten eine Erkältung. Wir gingen ins Bett. 7. Er war sehr reich. Er war sehr traurig. 8. Das Mädchen ging ins Bett. Sie war sehr müde. 9. Ich traf sie. Sie lächelte immer. 10. Ich öffnete die Schublade. Ich sah die Taschenuhr.

Exercise 45

It was raining when the fisherman rowed across (= over) the lake. He caught no fish (*plural*), as the fish were not hungry. My children were listening to the German children's songs on the wireless while I was writing this exercise. As soon as he comes home he will 'phone you. Did you not shut the doors before you went to bed? When I go[1] to Berlin I shall visit your uncle. As they were not at home we put the letter in the letter-box. It was snowing as we drove to the station. He speaks German, French, English and Italian, although he has never been in these countries. They worked until it was quite dark. When the maid came to the door the man asked for bread and tea. We went[1] by boat across the lake, although it was quite dark.

LESSON XVI

OTHER PRONOUNS

We must now learn the remaining personal pronouns:

1st Personal Pronoun

	Singular			Plural	
Nom.	ich	I		wir	we
Acc.	mich	me		uns	us
Dat.	mir	to me		uns	to us

2nd Personal Pronoun

	Singular				Plural	
Nom.	du	thou	Sie	you	ihr	
Acc.	dich	thee	Sie	you	euch	[2]
Dat.	dir	to thee	Ihnen	to you	euch	

He has told (to) me. Er hat mir gesagt.
He saw us. Er sah uns.
They saw you. Sie sahen Sie.
She gives (to) us a book. Sie gibt uns ein Buch.
Nobody saw me, but everybody saw you. Niemand sah mich, aber jedermann sah Sie.

---

[1] To go (in a car, train, or boat), fahren (by, mit).
[2] These forms are the real plural of du, dich, dir.

Indefinite Pronouns

1. *Man* is a very useful word corresponding to the English *one, we, they, people, you,* used indefinitely and not referring to any particular person:

> Man hat es mir gesagt. People have told me (*or* I have been told).

Man can only be used in the nominative. In other cases the following pronoun is used.

2. Einer refers indefinitely to a single person or thing:

> Einer meiner Freunde, one of my friends.
> Ich gehe zu einem Restaurant, wo die Kellner einen schnell bedienen. I go to a restaurant where the waiters serve one quickly.

The English *one* is untranslated in German after an adjective:

> Ich habe keine Feder. Haben Sie eine? I haven't a pen. Have you one?
> BUT: Hier ist eine gute. Here is a good one.

3. Keiner, niemand. Both mean *none, no one, nobody,* and keiner also *none* in speaking of things:

> Ich habe kein Brot, und du hast auch keines. I have no bread and you have none also.
> Niemand (keiner) hat uns gesehen. Nobody saw us.

Note. Both einer and keiner are declined like welcher or dieser. Niemand takes -s or -es in the genitive, and may (but need not) take -en in the accusative and -em in the dative. In this respect it is just like jemand, which follows.

4. Jemand means *somebody, someone.*

5. Wer means *he who, whoever,* and sends the verb to the end:

> Wer das gesagt hat, lügt. He who (whoever) said that is lying.

6. Nichts, *nothing,* etwas, *something.*

7. Welcher, *some, any.*

Ich habe keinen Zucker. Haben Sie welchen? I have no
sugar. Have you any?
Hast du kein warmes Wasser? Hier ist welches. Haven't
you any warm water? Here is some.

Indefinite Adjectives *or* Pronouns

The following may be used either as adjectives or
pronouns:

all, all (1)
ander-, ander, other (2)
beide, both
ein bißchen, a (very) little
ein paar, a few
einige, some, any (plur.)
etwas, some, any (sing.)
jeder, each, every, each one
genug, enough (3)

manch-, mancher, some, many,
  many a
mehr, more
mehrere, several
viel, much; (plur.), many (4)
wenig, little; (plur.), few (4)
keiner von beiden, neither
a few = einige or ein paar

1. Alles = *all, everything* (it may even replace alle (*pl.*)
meaning *all, everybody*). *Which* or *that* after alles is
rendered by was.

All the may be translated by "all" with the proper
ending or by "all" + article. Before words like *his, my,
this*, etc. "all" need not take an ending:

Alles, was er sagte. Everything he said.
Er stahl all das Geld. He stole all the money.
All meine Freunde. All my friends.

All = *the whole of* = der ganze:

Die ganze Stadt. All the town.

2. *Other* = *different*, ander-.
   Other = *additional*, noch (ein).

Dieses Buch ist nicht sehr gut. Haben Sie ein anderes?
This book is not very good. Have you another one?
Hier sind nur zwei Bücher. Haben Sie noch eines? Here
are only two books. Have you another (one)?

3. Genug can follow the noun:

Haben wir genug Zucker *or* Zucker genug? Have we enough
sugar?

4. In the singular viel and wenig need not take an ending. *A little* = ein wenig.

Vocabulary

die Mahlzeit, meal
das Frühstück, breakfast
das Mittagessen, lunch
das Abendessen, dinner
der Kaffee, coffee
das Brötchen, roll
die Butter, butter
der Käse,[1] cheese
die Milch, milk
die Suppe, soup
der Wein, wine
das Bier, beer
die Torte, cake
der Teller, plate
die Kanne, pot
der Speiseschrank, food-cup-
    board, larder, pantry
die Kartoffel, potato

die Karotte, carrot
die Bohne, bean
die Erbse, pea
das Eis, ice (cream)
das Bonbon (—s, —s), sweet
die Sahne, cream
die Kirsche, cherry
die Apfelsine, orange
die Banane, banana
die Zitrone, lemon
das Messer, knife
die Gabel, fork
der Löffel, spoon
die Tasse, cup
die Dose, bowl, basin, tin
pflücken, to pluck, gather,
    pick
schläfrig, sleepy

Exercise 46

Der Dieb antwortete mir nicht. Hast du sie nicht am Bahnhof getroffen? Wer hat Ihnen dieses schöne Buch gegeben? Es sind viele Kirschen und Äpfel im Garten. Ja, ich habe sie schon gesehen. Ich werde meinem Freunde welche geben. Meine kleine Schwester bat mich um Bonbons. Ich gab ihr einige, aber sie hat sie schon gegessen. "Noch ein Glas, bitte!" sagte ich zum Kellner, aber er hörte mich nicht. Zu Weihnachten wird Onkel Fritz uns besuchen. Wir haben noch etwas Butter im Speiseschrank. Essen Sie gern Brötchen mit Butter und Käse? Wir haben keine Apfelsinen mehr. Trinken Sie Kaffee mit oder ohne Sahne? Mit Sahne, wenn Sie welche haben. Beide Brüder (Die beiden Brüder) waren dort. Haben Sie keine anderen Bananen? Ich habe noch einige,[2] aber sie sind nicht reif. Ich werde dir ein Eis kaufen, wenn du mir einige Erbsen und

[1] 2nd Declension.
[2] noch einige (plur.), noch etwas (sing.), some more.

Bohnen im Garten pflückst. Hast du noch etwas Tee in der Kanne? Ist jemand an der Tür? Ich sehe niemanden dort. Man hat alles gehört, was du mir gestern sagtest. Jeder (Ein jeder) im Dorfe hat seinen langen Garten, worin er Kartoffeln, Bohnen, Erbsen, Äpfel, Kirschen usw. hat. Man trinkt viel Kaffee in Deutschland. Ich hatte keinen Teller, aber der Kellner hat mir einen gebracht.

Exercise 47

People drink more tea in England. Have you any coffee in the larder? Yes, I have a little. If you haven't enough books I have another one here. Our uncle gave us some sweets and oranges. I like oranges. The huntsman drank another glass of[1] wine. There are some more potatoes in the garden, if you have not enough here. The Spanish girls were picking oranges and lemons, and they gave us some. Have you any milk or cream? The breakfast at the "Blue Cow" was fairly cheap, but the lunch at the "Red Lion" was very dear, and they gave us no coffee. I do not like cheese. Is there any more sugar in the basin? The waiter has brought me another knife, as this one is dirty. For (zum) dinner we shall have cherries and bananas with cream. The waiter will bring you some more soup. Everybody was sleepy but nobody went to bed. All his friends are in America. A few sheep were in (auf) the field. He speaks a (very) little German, but no Spanish. Who has eaten all the cherries?

[1] *Of* in such expressions is omitted.

LESSON XVII

AUXILIARIES OF MOOD—THE IMPERATIVE

There are six very important little verbs that now claim attention. They are generally used along with the Infinitives of other verbs, and so are called Auxiliaries. Since they tell us something about the mode or manner in which an action is to be done, they are often called the Auxiliaries of *Mood*. You have already come across three of them in your reading.

	Infinitive	Imperfect	Past Part.	Pres. Ind.
to be permitted to dare	dürfen	durfte	gedurft	ich darf
to be able	können	konnte	gekonnt	ich kann
to be permitted to like	mögen	mochte	gemochte	ich mag
to be obliged to	müssen	mußte	gemußt	ich muß
to owe to, to be to	sollen	sollte	gesollt	ich soll
to be willing, to wish	wollen	wollte	gewollt	ich will

There is little difficulty in dealing with these verbs, as they are good-natured enough to be very regular. The Present Indicative of each is given below. You will observe that the plural is always the same as the Infinitive:

1. ich	darf, I may	kann, I can	mag, I may[1]
2. du	darfst	kannst	magst
3. er	darf	kann	mag
1. wir	dürfen	können	mögen
2. { Sie	dürfen	können	mögen
{ ihr	dürft	könnt	mögt
3. sie	dürfen	können	mögen

1. ich	muß, I must	soll, I am to	will, I will
2. du	mußt	sollst	willst
3. er	muß	soll	will
1. wir	müssen	sollen	wollen
2. { Sie	müssen	sollen	wollen
{ ihr	müßt	sollt	wollt or wollet
3. sie	müssen	sollen	wollen

[1] The student is advised to *avoid* the use of mögen at this stage.

For the other tenses these verbs are treated exactly like ordinary verbs. Thus the Perfect of müssen is ich habe gemußt = I have musted, *i.e.* I have been obliged to. But when these verbs are used with the Infinitive of another verb they take the form of the Infinitive instead of the Past Participle in the Perfect tenses. Thus "I have been obliged to wait" runs ich habe warten müssen.

The Imperative

When we order or command we are said to use the Imperative mood. Tanzen is *to dance*, tanze is the order *dance!* if given to one person, tanzet if to more than one person. These two forms are used only in addressing near relations, intimate friends and children.

The ordinary form of the Imperative, both in speaking to one person and to several persons, is tanzen Sie!

Singular (familiar)		Plural (familiar)	Singular and Plural (ordinary or polite form)
suche	seek	suchet	suchen Sie
lege	lay *or* place	leget	legen Sie
arbeite	work	arbeitet	arbeiten Sie
antworte	answer	antwortet	antworten Sie

Geben Sie mir ein Buch! Give me a book.
Senden Sie ihr den Vogel! Send her the bird.

Let us go.
{
Gehen wir!
Laß[1] uns gehen!
Wir wollen gehen.
}

See also p. 133.

Vocabulary

der Zug, train
der Autobus, bus
die Straßenbahn, tram

das Rad, wheel, (bike)
die Hupe, horn
die Bremse, brake

---

[1] It all depends on whom we are addressing:
Laß uns gehen! (du).
Lassen Sie uns gehen! (Sie).
Laßt uns gehen! (ihr).

die Straßenkreuzung, crossroads
die Tankstelle, petrol station
das Benzin, petrol
der Benzinbehälter, (petrol-)tank
das Motorrad, motor-cycle
eine Bootfahrt, a boat trip
die Taxe, taxi
gleich, immediately
rückwärts, backwards
gut, good, well
*besteigen, to board
winken, to beckon, signal
*verlassen, to leave
*rufen, to call, shout
fragen, to ask
das Fahrrad, bicycle
auf dem Fahrrad *fahren, to cycle
*radfahren, to cycle
der Reifen, tyre
der Verkehrspolizist, traffic policeman
zu Fuß *gehen,[1] to go on foot

die Einbahnstraße, one-way street
eine Radfahrt machen, to go for a cycle-ride[2]
eine Autofahrt, a car-ride
mit dem Zug *fahren,[3] to go by train
mit dem Flugzeug *fliegen,[3] to go by air
versäumen, to miss
platzen, to burst
*steigen, to mount, climb
*halten, to stop
in Ordnung, in order
parken, to park (vehicle)
das Parken ist verboten, parking is forbidden
überholen, to overtake
*scheinen, to shine, seem
langsam, slow, slowly
eilen, to hurry
der Weg, way
böse, bad

Exercise 48

Der Vater sagte zu den Kindern: "Wollt ihr heute nachmittag eine Autofahrt nach Berlin machen?" "O ja, gerne!" riefen die Kinder. Sie mußten ihre neuen Anzüge tragen, weil sie ihre Kusinen und Vettern in Berlin besuchen sollten. Sie konnten das Haus nicht vor drei Uhr verlassen, weil die Mutter nicht fertig war. "Kann ich nach Berlin auf dem Rad fahren?" fragte der kleine Karl. "O nein!" antwortete der Vater. "Auf dem Rad geht es viel zu langsam. Du mußt mit uns kommen."

Bald waren sie alle fertig. Der Vater kann sehr gut fahren. "Ich muß mehr Benzin kaufen," sagte er, "der Benzinbehälter ist fast leer." Also hielten sie an einer Tankstelle. Dann kamen sie an eine Straßenkreuzung. Dort war rotes Licht, und sie mußten warten. Herrn

---

[1] Gehen strictly speaking is *to walk*, and when a vehicle is mentioned or implied, fahren should be used.

[2] Similarly with Autofahrt, Bootfahrt.

[3] To travel *by* is in German to drive or fly *with*.

Schmidts Auto kann sehr gut steigen, und sie fuhren sehr schnell auf dem Wege nach Berlin. Um halb vier waren sie in Berlin. Dort sahen sie einen armen Motorradfahrer, der einen geplatzten Reifen reparierte. Auf den breiten Straßen Berlins sahen sie Autobusse, Straßenbahnen, Autos, Taxen und Fahrräder. Dort ist der Verkehr sehr gefährlich. Sie fuhren in eine Einbahnstraße, also mußten sie rückwärts fahren. Über der Stadt sahen sie ein großes Flugzeug, das nach Amerika fliegen sollte. Viele Fußgänger eilten über die Straße, und es war gut, daß die Hupe in Ordnung war. Aber sie konnten immer ziemlich schnell fahren und überholten viele andere Autos. Dann hielt das Auto, und Herr Schmidt winkte einem Verkehrspolizisten. Er hat nach[1] dem Wege fragen müssen. Bald aber waren sie vor dem Hause des Onkels.

Exercise 49

You can go to Berlin if you want to. I am to go to the dentist this evening. May[2] I smoke here? I will[3] take my dog for a walk in the park. He was to fly to Paris yesterday (= yesterday to Paris), but suddenly became ill. We had to walk home. As he could not speak German he took me with (him). You are to go immediately to bed. German is spoken here (= here one speaks German). Shall[4] I buy some bread? You are to talk to (= to speak with) nobody. We could not see the aeroplane on account of the fog. May we go to the cinema this evening? We had to go by taxi. If the weather is warm you may bathe in the lake this afternoon (= this afternoon in the lake—always *Time* before *Place*). We want to see your cows and sheep. I can-

[1] To ask for = to demand, bitten um; = to inquire about, fragen nach.

[2] *May* in questions and negative statements: use dürfen.

[3] When *will* means *want to* rather than just a future action, use wollen.

[4] When *shall* has the meaning of *am I to*, use sollen.

not tell you (it). As my brother is unable to visit you, he is sending you a letter.

Exercise 50

Take (= bring) this letter to the post. Let us go for a walk round the town. I have had[1] to go to Berlin. She has had to learn Spanish. They have not been able to find your book. He is to leave London tomorrow (Time before Place!). Have you (du) been able to see this film? He would not (= did not want to) answer. My sisters had to go by air (= fly with the aeroplane). I cannot speak Swedish. Can she speak Dutch? We have not been able to send you many apples, as the summer has been too bad. We could not travel very quickly, on account of the fog. You can go by bus to the station. Will you sing us a song? I cannot sing, as I have a bad cold.

Exercise 51

Kellner,[2] bringen Sie uns zwei Glas[3] Bier, bitte! Chauffeur, fahren Sie schnell zum Bahnhof! Geben Sie mir bitte ein Eis. Gehen wir ins Kino! Bitte, wiegen Sie diesen Brief für mich! Reichen Sie mir bitte den Zucker! Laßt uns heute abend ins Theater gehen! Öffnen Sie bitte die Tür! Frage den Schutzmann (den Polizisten) nach dem Wege! Wir wollen morgen nach London fahren! Bitte, sagen Sie mir, wo ich eine Taxe finden kann. Kaufen Sie mir einige Zigaretten! Geben Sie mir eine Londoner Zeitung!

[1] *I have had to* may be rendered either by ich habe . . . sollen or ich habe . . . müssen. Sollen implies *duty* or *obligation*, müssen indicates *necessity*.

[2] It is customary to address a waiter as Ober! or Herr Ober! (Oberkellner, strictly speaking, is the *head waiter*, but in calling a waiter this form of flattery is adopted.)

[3] Notice that in such expressions, where the English *of* is omitted, a *masculine* or *neuter* noun does not take the plural form. A *feminine* noun does, *e.g.*

zwei Flaschen Wein, two bottles of wine (die Flasche, *bottle*).

LESSON XVIII

SEPARABLE AND INSEPARABLE VERBS

1. The Separable Prefix

In English we have the word *upset*. This is composed of two separate words, *up* and *set*. But we cannot separate these words without changing the meaning of the whole. *Set up* means something very different from *upset*.

Now in German we have two kinds of verbs made up of a verb and another word. To the first class belong what are called separable verbs, because the two parts can be separated; the others are called inseparable, because the two parts must always be kept together.

The peculiarities of separable verbs are these:

1. In the Present and Imperfect Indicative and in the Imperative the separable little word is taken away from the front of the verb and put at the end of the sentence. Thus, zurückkommen means *to come back*; so we have the sentence, da kamen wir nach London zurück. In the same way, kommen Sie zurück means *come back*.

2. In the Past Participle and in the Infinitive the ge- and zu- are put between the two parts of separable verbs, losgelassen and zurückzukommen. Er wünschte zurückzukommen = he wished to come back.

3. In pronouncing the word more stress is laid upon the separable part, thus: zurück'kommen, los'lassen.

Here are some separable verbs to practise on:

*ankommen, to arrive	*einsteigen, to get in (vehicle)
*aufstehen, to get up	*wegnehmen, to take away
*ausgehen, to go out	abreisen, to set out
*fortfahren, to go on	zumachen, to shut

It is to be noted that separable verbs do not separate their prefix unless in *independent* sentences. I come back soon = ich komme bald zurück. But for "if I come back soon" we write, wenn ich bald zurückkomme.

2. The Inseparable Prefix

The very fact that certain verbs are called *separable* leads us to expect that certain other verbs are called *inseparable*. Those inseparable verbs are made up of two parts just like the separable, but the prefixes are never separated from the rest of the verb. The prefixes that cannot be separated from the rest of the verb are: be-, emp-, ent-, er-, ge-, hinter-, miß-, ver-, voll-, wider-, zer-.

*behalten, to keep
*empfangen, to receive
*entscheiden, to decide
*erschrecken, to be frightened (vor, at)
gebrauchen, to use, employ

*hinterlassen, to leave
*mißfallen, to displease
*vergessen, to forget
*vollbringen, to accomplish
*widerstehen, to resist
*zerbrechen, to break

Besides the quality which gives them their name—that of retaining the prefixes joined to the verb in all cases—these inseparable verbs have the following three characteristics:

1. They do not admit of the prefix ge- in the Past Participle. We say ich habe vergessen (not gevergessen).

2. The zu of the Infinitive is put before the prefix: as zu mißhandeln.

3. The accent is placed not on the prefix but on the root part of the verb.

3. Some Special Cases

There are four prefixes—durch-, über-, unter- and um—that give a good deal of trouble, because they are sometimes separable and sometimes inseparable.

The test is: Does the preposition have its usual meaning along with the verb? If it has, the compound is a separable verb; if it has not, the compound is an inseparable verb. Umgehen may mean "to go about", "to lounge about", "to go round". In these cases um- has clearly retained its ordinary meaning, so it is separable. I go about with my neighbour = ich gehe mit meinem Nachbar um, *i.e.* I associate with him. But umgehen also means to elude, to avoid. Here um- has not its literal meaning: it is used figuratively, so the verb is inseparable. I avoid it = ich umgehe es.

In actual speech the separable forms accent the durch-, über-, unter- and um-, the inseparables accent the root of the verb. Thus: ü'bersetzen = to set over; über-se'tzen = to translate.

The inseparables form one class of verbs that do not have ge- in the Past Participle. There is another, and rather an important class. If any new verb comes into English we at once make it into a regular verb by adding *-ed* for both Past and Past Participle: *Telegraph, telegraphed, telegraphed*. The Germans just as naturally make the verb end in -ieren and we have telegrafieren, telegrafierte, telegrafiert; so with *telephone*: telefonieren, telefonierte, telefoniert. Most new German verbs, especially those derived from the classical languages and from the French, end in -ieren; and all German verbs ending in -ieren have no ge- in the Past Participle, and have the ordinary -te in the Past: studieren, studierte, studiert = to study; marschieren, marschierte, marschiert = to march. The reason for the omission of the ge- is that in these verbs, and in inseparable verbs, the first syllable is not accented.

Notice carefully the order of the separable prefix:

Ich gehe	jeden Tag	aus.	I go out every day.
Ich ging	,,	aus.	I went out every day.
Ich bin	,,	ausgegangen.	I have been out every day.
Ich werde	,,	ausgehen.	I shall go out every day.
Ich will	,,	ausgehen.	I want to go out every day.
Ich wünsche	,,	auszugehen.	I desire to go out every day.
Da ich	,,	ausging.	As I went out every day.

The Particles Hin and Her

These particles are frequently added to form a compound with the verb or with a separable prefix in order further to define the *direction*.

Hin expresses a *direction away* from the point of view, her a *Movement towards* it. Everything depends on the point from which we "project" the description. For instance, if we describe a man walking along the street and say he entered a house, we may take the point of view of the man in the street and say hin, or the point of view inside the house and say her.

These particles are very important and should be constantly studied and practised.

Note the following:

> (Kommen Sie) herein! Come in! (Einkommen is *to come in, enter*.)
> Gehen Sie hinaus! Go out! (Ausgehen, *to go out*.)
> Wir gingen die Straße hinauf. We went up the street.
> Er kam die Straße herunter. He came down the street.

It follows that a person going anywhere will himself say hin, as he must be going to a place away from him, and a verb like kommen usually takes her.

The English *there* and *where*

These particles are often used to complete the sense of direction, a fine point that is often lacking in English. The words *there* and *where* are therefore dort (da) or dorthin (dahin), wo or wohin, according as the meaning is *there* (in that place) or *thither* (to that place), or *where* (in what place) or *whither* (to what place):

> Wohin gehen Sie (Wo gehen Sie hin)? Where are you going?
> Wo ist das Buch? Where is the book?
> Er ging dorthin. He went there.
> Er steht dort. He is standing there.
> Er legte das Buch hin. He put the book down.
> Der Junge fiel hin. The boy fell (down).

Vocabulary

das Gepäck, luggage
der Träger, porter
der Gepäckraum, cloak-room
der Erfrischungsraum, refreshment-room
der Schaffner, guard
die Lokomotive, engine
der Wagen, carriage
das Abteil, compartment
das Raucherabteil, smoking compartment
das Nichtraucherabteil, non-smoking compartment
der Schalter, ticket-office
die Rolltreppe, escalator
die (Fahr)karte, ticket
die Bahnsteigkarte, platform ticket
die Hinfahrtskarte, single (ticket)
die Rückfahrkarte, return (ticket)
der Anschluß, connection
der Speisewagen, dining-car
*lassen, to leave (thing)
*verlassen, to leave (person or place)
frei, free, vacant
besetzt, occupied, taken
abholen, to meet (from the station)
*fahren, to run (of trains)
*pfeifen, to whistle
rechtzeitig, punctual(ly)
Einsteigen! Take your seats, please!
*zurückgehen, to go back, return
*lesen, to read

sonst, otherwise
der Automat, ticket-machine
der Gepäckwagen, luggage-van
der Platz, place, seat
der Abort, lavatory
der Gang, corridor
das Netz, rack
der Ausgang, exit
der Wartesaal, waiting-room
der Bücherstand, bookstall
der Bahnsteig, platform
das Trinkgeld, "tip"
der Koffer, suit-case
das Köfferchen, attaché-case
der D-Zug,[1] through-train
der Zuschlag, extra (charge)
der Schlafwagen, sleeping-car
der Aufenthalt, stop
der Fahrplan, timetable
der Schnellzug, fast train
der Eckplatz, corner-seat
*eintreten, to enter
*einsteigen, to enter (vehicle)
sich hinauslehnen, to lean out
*ankommen, to arrive
*abfahren, to leave, depart (of vehicle)
*aussteigen, to alight
*umsteigen, to change
holen, to fetch
versäumen, to miss
verspätet, delayed, late
zeigen, to show
furchtbar, terribly
Alles umsteigen! All change!
*zurückkommen, to come back, return
gähnen, to yawn
hinsetzen, to put down

Exercise 52

Müllers[2] wollten nach Köln fahren. Sie suchten einen Schnellzug im Fahrplan. Ihr Gepäck war fertig. Sie fuhren mit der Taxe zum Bahnhof. Herr Müller kaufte

---

[1] = Durchgangszug.
[2] The Millers.

die Karten am Schalter. Sie mußten zum Bahnsteig neun eilen. Der Gepäckträger trug das Gepäck. Hilde kaufte einige Bonbons, und Frau Müller wählte vom Bücherstand einige Zeitungen. Weil der Zug verspätet war, warteten sie ein bißchen im Wartesaal. Dann fuhr der Zug herein. Der Träger setzte das Gepäck in den Gepäckwagen, und Herr Müller gab ihm ein Trinkgeld. Sie stiegen alle in ein leeres Abteil ein. Hilde und Max wählten die Eckplätze, weil sie zum Fenster hinaussehen wollten. Herr Müller legte sein Köfferchen auf das Netz.

Die Lokomotive pfiff, und dann fuhren sie ab. Da sie in einem Raucherabteil waren, begann Herr Müller zu rauchen. Er raucht gern Zigaretten. In Aachen[1] mußten sie umsteigen. Um halb eins gingen sie den Gang entlang[2] zum Speisewagen. Nach dem Mittagessen gingen sie zu ihrem Abteil zurück. Max mußte zum Abort gehen, weil seine Hände furchtbar schmutzig waren. Herr Müller gähnte. Er war müde und begann zu schlafen. Als sie rechtzeitig in Köln ankamen, stiegen sie schnell aus. Auf dem Bahnsteig sahen sie Onkel Otto und Tante Gisela. Ein Träger holte ihr Gepäck vom Gepäckwagen. Herr Müller gab die Karten ab, und sie verließen den Bahnhof. Sie fuhren eine lange, enge Straße hinauf und kamen am Hause des Onkels an. Sie traten ins Haus ein. Sie waren alle müde und hungrig.

Exercise 53

Give me three singles for (nach) Berlin, please! Do not lean out of the window! Porter, take my luggage to the fast train for Cologne, please. Driver (Taxi), drive quickly to the station, otherwise I shall miss the train for Coblence (Koblenz). Must I change in Aix-la-Chapelle? I left the house at half-past six.[3] All the seats were occupied. We returned last Monday to

[1] Aix-la-Chapelle.
[2] Entlang, *along*, follows the noun in the accusative.
[3] um halb sieben.

Berlin. Is there (omit *there*) a seat vacant for me? The
through-train leaves at 9.30.[1] Aunt Marie met her at
(von) the station. Did you miss the connection at
Kassel? A tall man entered the room and spoke to (with)
me. My hat is in the dining-car. If you travel by this
fast train you will have to pay extra. Put your case
down. Where are you going? Where have you put
your gloves? Where are the tickets?

LESSON XIX

CARDINAL NUMBERS

We have already had the numbers from one up to
twenty. Now we must have the others. Old-fashioned
people among ourselves still say *five-and-twenty* for 25.
This is the regular way in German.

21	einundzwanzig	50	fünfzig
22	zweiundzwanzig	53	dreiundfünfzig
23	dreiundzwanzig	60	sechzig (note the s omitted)
24	vierundzwanzig	64	vierundsechzig
25	fünfundzwanzig	70	siebzig
26	sechsundzwanzig	75	fünfundsiebzig
27	siebenundzwanzig	80	achtzig
28	achtundzwanzig	86	sechsundachtzig
29	neunundzwanzig	90	neunzig
30	dreißig	97	siebenundneunzig
31	einunddreißig	100	hundert
40	vierzig	101	hundert und eins
42	zweiundvierzig	102	hundert und zwei

The hundreds go quite regularly, zweihundert, dreihundert, vierhundert, and so on. So with the thousands:
tausend = 1 000, zweitausend = 2 000, dreitausend =
3 000, etc. In a general way *a* hundred and *a* thousand
are simply hundert and tausend *without* the ein. But if
we want to speak of one hundred or one thousand we say

---

[1] um halb zehn.

einhundert and eintausend (one word in each case) respectively. A million is eine Million (with accent on the on).

Here follow some examples of big numbers expressed in words:

123 = hundert dreiundzwanzig.
947 = neunhundert siebenundvierzig.
304 = dreihundert und vier.
1 032 = ein) tausend zweiunddreißig.
1 870 = (ein) tausend achthundert siebzig or achtzehnhundert (und) siebzig.
1 900 = (ein) tausend neunhundert or neunzehnhundert.
1 563 825 = eine Million fünfhundertdreiundsechzigtausend achthundert fünfundzwanzig.

Hundert and tausend when used alone (*i.e.* not as adjectives) are regarded as nouns, and form their plural nominative and accusative by adding -e and dative by adding -en.

The simple arithmetical processes are as follows:

zweimal drei ist sechs $= 2 \times 3 = 6$
drei und vier ist sieben $= 3 + 4 = 7$
neun geteilt durch drei ist drei $= 9 :^{1} 3 = 3$
dreißig weniger zwanzig ist zehn $= 30 - 20 = 10$

ORDINAL NUMBERS

The numbers we have been dealing with up till now are called *cardinal* numbers, because all other numbers *hinge* upon them—*cardo, cardinis*, being Latin for a *hinge*. But we sometimes want to express the *order* in which things occur, and then we use what are called the *ordinal* numbers—first, second, third, fourth, fifth, sixth, etc. You note that the first three end differently from all the rest. Just as we make a cardinal number into an ordinal by adding -*th*, so the Germans do the same thing by adding -te. Thus vierte, fünfte, sechste, and so on up to neunzehnte. 1st and 3rd are irregular, erste and dritte; 2nd is quite regular, zweite.

From 20 onwards all the numbers add -ste: 20th =

----
[1] This is the German division sign (our ÷).

zwanzigste; 90th = neunzigste; 100th = hundertste; 1,000th = tausendste.

But if a large number ends with a German number between one and nineteen inclusive it ends in -te: 112th = hundertundzwölfte; 1,010th = tausendundzehnte.

The -te or the -ste are the ordinary endings of adjectives, and only the parts of numbers which have these terminations are declined.

> He has chosen the 101st man.   Er hat den hundertundersten Mann gewählt.
> His fifth attempt, sein fünfter Versuch.

There are certain very useful terminations used in connection with numbers:

1. -erlei when added means of so many kinds: zweierlei, dreierlei, achterlei, hunderterlei = of two kinds, of three kinds, of eight kinds, of a hundred kinds respectively; allerlei = of all kinds; vielerlei = of many kinds.

2. -mal means so many times: einmal = once; fünfmal = five times; zehnmal = ten times; tausendmal = a thousand times.

3. -fach means so many fold: einfach = onefold (it also means *simple*); vierfach = fourfold; hundertfach = a hundredfold.

4. -ns when added to the ordinal numbers gives meanings corresponding to our "-ly" in numbers: erstens = firstly; zweitens = secondly; sechstens = sixthly, and so on.

5. -l when added to the ordinals gives the forms corresponding to our fractions: das Drittel = the third; das Viertel = the fourth; das Sechstel = the sixth; das Dreißigstel = the thirtieth; das Hundertstel = the hundredth. $\frac{3}{4}$ = drei Viertel; $\frac{5}{7}$ = fünf Siebentel; $\frac{13}{20}$ = dreizehn Zwanzigstel.

DATES AND LETTERS

In order to deal with dates we must learn the names of the days of the week and the months of the year.

Das Jahr = the year; der Monat = the month; die Woche = the week.

January	Januar	May	Mai	September	Septem'ber
February	Februar	June	Juni	October	Okto'ber
March	März	July	Juli	November	Novem'ber
April	April'	August	August'	December	Dezem'ber

Sunday Sonntag	Tuesday	Dienstag	Thursday	Donnerstag
Monday Montag	Wednesday	Mittwoch	Friday	Freitag

Saturday Samstag or Sonnabend

Our English way of saying *of a Sunday* or *on Sundays* is represented in German by merely adding an -s to the day of the week we refer to.

On before a day of the week is translated an dem, contracted into am: am Samstag = on Saturday; am Sonntag = on Sunday.

The words for the months and days are all masculine in German, as are also the words for the four seasons.

Spring, der Frühling	Autumn, der Herbst
Summer, der Sommer	Winter, der Winter

In before a month or a season is translated by in dem, contracted into im: im Juli = in July; im Frühling = in spring.

But if we express a particular day of the month we use am. Thus:

On the 5th of November, am fünften November.
On the 18th of June in the year 1815, am achtzehnten Juni im Jahre achtzehnhundert fünfzehn.

Dates are also expressed by the accusative of the article without a preposition, as: den vierten Juli = on the 4th of July.

The hours of the day are represented by a numeral and the feminine word Uhr always in the singular: 11 o'clock = elf Uhr; 4 o'clock = vier Uhr. We know that auf means *direction towards* and nach means *after*, so we are not surprised to find that ein Viertel auf sechs and ein Viertel nach fünf mean the same thing: *a quarter past five.* Similarly, drei Viertel auf drei and ein Viertel vor drei both can stand for a quarter to three. Scottish students will recognise an old friend in the phrase halb vier = half-four: this means half *towards* four, and therefore means half-past three. The most usual way with minutes is to use the number with nach up to the half-hour *past*, and the number with vor from the half-hour up to the next hour. Thus: 4.25 p.m. will be nachmittags um fünfundzwanzig Minuten nach vier; 4.35 a.m. will be morgens um fünfundzwanzig Minuten vor fünf. When anything is done *at* a certain time we use the preposition um, as um zehn Uhr = at 10 o'clock. The question, *What o'clock is it?* is put Wieviel Uhr ist es?

The student should endeavour to get into touch with a German living in Germany who would be willing to correspond with him. This gives an added interest to his studies and by correcting each other's mistakes the correspondence can be beneficial to both sides.

How to begin a letter:

(Die Adresse)
den 15. Juli 1971.

(Die Anschrift):

Lieber Karl!	Dear Charles,
Mein lieber Heinrich!	My dear Henry,
Liebe Käthi!	Dear Kathleen,
Meine liebste Ottilie!	My dearest Ottilie,

Not so intimate:

Lieber Herr Klein!	Dear Mr. Small,
Liebe Frau Schmidt!	Dear Mrs. Smith,
Sehr geehrtes Fräulein Braun!	Dear Miss Brown,
Geehrter Herr Doktor!	Dear Doctor ——.

Besten (Schönen) Dank für Ihren Brief (Ihre Karte) vom 3. März. Many thanks for your letter (card) of the 3rd March.

Ihren interessanten Brief vom 9. April habe ich gestern erhalten. Besten Dank! I received your interesting letter of the 9th April yesterday. Many thanks.

Ich lege Ihnen hiermit ein neues Bild von mir (von meinem Haus, von meinem Hund) bei. I enclose a new photo of myself (of my house, my dog).

How to end a letter:

Mit schönem Gruß an Sie und Ihre werte Frau, with best
    wishes to you and your wife.
Meine Schwester läßt Sie herzlich grüßen, my sister sends
    you her kind regards.
Mit den freundlichsten Grüßen, with sincerest wishes.
In der Hoffnung, bald im Besitz Ihrer Antwort zu sein.
    Hoping to get your answer shortly.

Ihr (Stets Ihr),   Yours truly (sincerely),
        N.   N.

More formal and business-like:

Hochachtungsvoll,   Yours faithfully,
        J. B.   J. B.

b.w.! = bitte wenden! = P.T.O.
N.S. (or P.S.) = P.S.

How to address the envelope:

> Herrn O. Hasenwinkel,
>   Recklinghausen,
>   Kellerstraße 13.

> Fräulein Ottilie Weißdorn,
>   bei Herrn Dr. Leineweber,
>   Rostock,
>   Wilhelmstr. 10.

Bitte nachsenden!   Please forward.
Eilt sehr!   Urgent!
Wenn unbestellbar, zurück an N.   In case of non-delivery,
    please return to N.

Exercise 54

Write in full or read quickly:

(a) $2 \times 3 = ?$ $5 + 3 = ?$
        $4 \times 5 = ?$ $9 + 6 = ?$
        $5 \times 6 = ?$ $19 + 17 = ?$
        $7 \times 3 = ?$ $13 + 14 = ?$
        $11 \times 11 = ?$ $43 + 38 = ?$

$$27: 3 = ?$$
$$81: 9 = ?$$
$$44: 4 = ?$$
$$121:11 = ?$$
$$250:50 = ?$$

$$98 - 57 = ?$$
$$139 - 87 = ?$$
$$1\,716 - 741 = ?$$
$$3\,921 - 1\,964 = ?$$
$$1\,888 - 777 = ?$$

(b) Um

9.0	6.30	12.0	1.40
2.45	3.20	12.10	10.45
11.10	3.50	1.0	5.30
5.45	7.15	1.20	8.15

(c) $\frac{1}{3}$, $\frac{8}{5}$, $\frac{4}{9}$, $\frac{1}{2}$, $\frac{3}{4}$, $\frac{5}{8}$, $\frac{6}{25}$;

1st, 2nd, 6th, 8th, 7th, 11th, 12th, 18th, 24th, 17th, 30th, 29th, 100th, 1000th.

LESSON XX

COMPARISON

When we compare two things in English we are said to use the *Comparative* degree of the adjective. I am stronger than you: here *stronger* is the Comparative, and is clearly formed by merely adding -*er* to the ordinary form of the adjective. In German we do exactly the same. Stark means *strong*, and we have already used stärker for *stronger*. Ich bin stärker als Sie = I am stronger than you. In addition to adding -er, however, the Germans (in the case of monosyllables) generally modify the vowel if it happens to be a, o, or u.

When more than two things are compared, we use what is called the *Superlative* degree of the adjective. This is indicated in English by the ending -*est*, as in *strongest*; the German ending is practically the same as in English; it is -st. Thus: *strongest* should be stärkst, but since the Superlative is always used with the article

or some demonstrative word it never in practice ends
baldly in -st, but must have the usual termination of an
adjective used attributively.

> Der stärkste Mann, the strongest man.
> Mein stärkster Freund, my strongest friend.
> Dieser Mann ist am stärksten, this man is strongest.

When an adjective ends in d, t, s, ß, sch or z, or a
vowel, there is an e put in before the st, making it
exactly like English: hart = hard; härtest = hardest;
treu, faithful, treuest, most faithful.

The ordinary form of the adjective is called the
Positive; so we have the following table drawn up under
three heads:

	Positive	Comparative	Superlative		
poor	arm	ärmer	(der or die or das)		ärmste
old	alt	älter	,,	,,	älteste
broad	breit	breiter	,,	,,	breiteste
stupid	dumm	dümmer	,,	,,	dümmste
noble	edel	edler	,,	,,	edelste
early	früh	früher	,,	,,	früheste
bad	schlecht	schlechter	,,	,,	schlechteste
brave	tapfer	tapf(e)rer	,,	,,	tapferste

Note that adjectives ending in -el, -en, -er leave out
the e in the Comparative. The -er and the -en adjectives
may keep the e, but the -el ones usually drop it. The
best plan is to drop it always in all three cases, and thus
save confusion.

The following one-syllabled adjectives do *not* take the
Umlaut in comparison:

false	falsch	falscher	falschest
glad	froh	froher	frohest
clear	klar	klarer	klarst
slim	schlank	schlanker	schlankst
flat	flach	flacher	flachst
bald	kahl	kahler	kahlst
round	rund	runder	rundest
proud	stolz	stolzer	stolzest
full	voll	voller	vollst
true	wahr	wahrer	wahrst
tender	zart	zarter	zartest

In German, as in all languages, some of the commonest adjectives are quite irregular. The following list should be learnt thoroughly:

	Positive	Comparative	Superlative		
good	gut	besser	(der or die or das)		beste
great	groß	größer	,,	,,	größte
high	hoch[1]	höher	,,	,,	höchste
near	nahe	näher	,,	,,	nächste

We have seen already that adjectives are frequently used as adverbs; and now we have to call attention to a peculiar adverbial form of the Superlative that may be called the Absolute Superlative, and is used predicatively with the verb sein. It has always the same form, and its termination does not change: am besten = the best; am größten = the greatest; am edelsten = the noblest. You will understand its use from the following examples:

> She is the most beautiful lady in the town. Sie ist die schönste Dame in der Stadt.
> This lady is most beautiful in the morning. Diese Dame ist morgens am schönsten.
> The just way is the best. Der gerade Weg ist der beste.
> This way is best in spring. Dieser Weg ist im Frühling am besten.

It is plain that the am besten form is used when there is really no comparison with other things in the same sentence. It states that the quality of the adjective exists in the highest degree in the subject of the sentence. In this form there is no noun implied as following the adjective, whereas in the der beste form there is an implied noun: der gerade Weg ist der beste (Weg).

There are three kinds of comparison, each of which deserves attention:

1. Comparison indicating *equality*: this is expressed by (eben) so . . . wie.

---

[1] When an e follows, the c is always omitted:

> Ein hoher Baum, a tall tree.
> Ein höherer Baum, a taller tree.

I am as good as you.   Ich bin so gut wie Sie.
The boy was as brave as his father.   Der Knabe war ebenso
tapfer wie sein Vater.

2. Comparison involving *inferiority* in respect of the
quality indicated by the adjective.   In this case we use
the form nicht so . . . wie; *i.e.* the eben is omitted.

You are not so bad as she.   Sie sind nicht so schlecht wie sie.
He is not as clever as his sister.   Er ist nicht so geschickt
wie seine Schwester.

3. Comparison involving *superiority* in respect of the
quality indicated by the adjective.   This is the commonest form, and is expressed by the ordinary comparative
followed by als.

The son was stronger than his father.   Der Sohn war stärker
als sein Vater.

4. When two adjectives refer to the same subject, the
form with mehr is usual:

He is more sly than clever.   Er ist mehr schlau als klug.

The peculiar expression, *the* so-and-so *the* so-and-so, is
expressed in German by je . . . desto or je . . . je.

The older a man is the wiser he is.   Je älter ein Mann ist,
desto klüger ist er.

Note the construction; je requires the verb to be thrown
to the end, desto requires inversion of verb.

The more the better, je mehr desto besser.
The longer the better, je länger je lieber.

When there is only one *the* with the comparative it is
rendered by desto or um so.

The better for you, desto besser für Sie, *or* um so besser für
Sie.

The Adverb

Many adverbs (saying how a thing is done) have the
same form as the corresponding adjectives, *e.g.*:

Das Mädchen ist schön.   The girl is *beautiful*.
Das Mädchen schreibt schön.   The girl writes *beautifully*.

The Comparison of the Adverb

{ schön	{ schöner	{ am schönsten
{ beautifully	{ more beautifully	{ most beautifully

Four irregular adverbs are worth learning here:

	Positive	Comparative	Superlative
soon	bald	eher or früher	am ehesten
willingly	gern	lieber	am liebsten
much	viel	mehr	am meisten
little	wenig	{ weniger	am wenigsten
		{ minder	am mindesten

Vocabulary

die Erde, earth	schnell, quick, fast
die Themse, Thames	süß, sweet, sweetly
das Gold, gold	vorsichtig, careful(ly)
das Eisen, iron	glücklich, happy, fortunate
die Luft, air	tief, deep
der Elefant, elephant	komisch, funny
der Schmetterling, butterfly	nett, nice (persons)
die Schwalbe, swallow	fleißig, industrious(ly)
der Eiffelturm, Eiffel Tower	faul, lazy
der Dom, cathedral	angenehm, pleasant
scharf, sharp	unangenehm, unpleasant
*aussehen, to look	*vorkommen, to seem
wieviel? how much?	kosten, to cost

Exercise 55

From the following "skeletons" make up comparisons, thus:

Die Maus, klein, der Hund.
Die Maus ist kleiner als der Hund.

London, groß, die Vereinigten Staaten. Die Erde, klein, die Sonne. Die Themse, lang, der Rhein. Paris, alt, Rom. Gold, hart, Eisen. Die Stadt, groß, das Dorf. Luft, schwer, Wasser. Der Elefant, stark, der Mann. Die Katze, falsch, der Hund. Der Knabe, klug, das Mädchen. Der Schmetterling, schnell, die Schwalbe. Die See, tief, der See. Der Eiffelturm, hoch, der Kölner Dom.

Exercise 56

Wieviel kosten diese Äpfel? Sind diese Kirschen teurer als die anderen? Diese sind am teuersten. Marie ist das netteste Mädchen im Dorf. Ottilie singt schön, Hilde singt schöner, aber Else singt am schönsten. Welcher Junge ist am klügsten? Otto ist der klügste, aber Konrad ist fast ebenso klug. Ist Belgien nicht so groß wie Holland? Dieses Mädchen ist ebenso hübsch wie ihre[1] Schwester. Je älter ein Mann wird, desto weniger kann er lernen. Ein höherer Baum als dieser ist in unserem Garten. Können Sie Deutsch (sprechen)? Ja? Um so besser. Je früher wir ankommen, desto länger werden wir warten müssen. Je mehr er trank, desto durstiger wurde er. Diese Fahrräder sind am besten. Otto ist der größte Junge in der Klasse. Es ist angenehmer hier im Garten als im Hause. Irmgard ist fleißiger als ihr Bruder. Wir müssen vorsichtiger durch diesen Nebel fahren. Diese Kirschen sind die süßesten. Der Garten sieht im Sommer hübscher aus als im Winter.

Exercise 57

The more industriously he works, the more he learns. The water is colder today than yesterday. It is getting (werden) darker. It was getting slowly lighter (brighter). Otto is tall, Konrad is taller, and Wilhelm is the tallest. Marie sings more sweetly than her sister. Are you as lazy as your brother? This boy does not look as clever as his brother. The longer we wait here, the darker it will be when we go back home. I have very little, she has less and her cousin (girl) has least. This dog is the most faithful. Is that knife sharper than this? I shall buy the biggest and sweetest apples. The teacher will give this book to the cleverest schoolboy.

[1] Grammatically, seine should be used, but ihre is more common with das Mädchen and das Fräulein.

LESSON XXI

POSSESSIVE AND CORRELATIVE PRONOUNS

In old-fashioned English we could say *mine* host, *mine* inn, *mine* enemy, but now we always say *my*. *My, thy, our, their, her, your,* always demand a noun to follow them, while *mine, thine, ours, theirs, hers, yours,* can do without a noun, but insist upon having a verb. *My* book, but the book is *mine*; *your* house, but this house is *yours*.

When the possessive is used as a pronoun it can be represented in two ways:

1. By—

Singular			Plural
meiner (m)	meine (f)	meines (n)	meine (all genders)

These forms are treated exactly like ordinary adjectives used without any article.

> Dein Vater ist arm, meiner ist reich.   Thy father is poor, mine is rich.
> Das ist nicht sein Buch, es ist meines.   That is not his book, it is mine.

2. By using the following form with the definite article:

Singular			Plural	
All genders			All genders	
(der, die or das)	meinige	mine	(die)	meinigen
,,	,, deinige	thine	,,	deinigen
,,	,, seinige	his *or* its	,,	seinigen
,,	,, ihrige	hers *or* its	,,	ihrigen
,,	,, unsrige	ours	,,	unsrigen
,,	,, eurige	yours	,,	eurigen
,,	,, Ihrige	yours	,,	Ihrigen
,,	,, ihrige	theirs	,,	ihrigen

The above is the form that is used in comparisons. You will gather its meaning from the following examples:

> Ihr Haus ist älter als das unsrige.   Your house is older than ours.
> Mein Freund ist ebenso arm wie der seinige.   My friend is as poor as his.

Unsere Straße ist nicht so breit wie die ihrige.   Our street is
not so wide as theirs.

Ihre Zähne sind schärfer als die meinigen.   Your teeth are
sharper than mine.

Zu meinem Vater und dem seinigen.   To my father and his.

From this last example it is clear that meinige and the
rest are used just like ordinary adjectives with the
definite article:

In unserer Stadt und in der Ihrigen.   In our city and in
yours.

Derjenige means *that* or *the one*, and may either go
with a noun or stand alone.   This is how it is declined;
it is always written as one word:

	Singular		Plural
Masculine	Feminine	Neuter	All genders
derjenige	diejenige	dasjenige	diejenigen
denjenige	diejenige	dasjenige	diejenigen
desjenigen	derjenigen	desjenigen	derjenigen
demjenigen	derjenigen	demjenigen	denjenigen

Diejenigen, welche = those who (such as).

He who has come is not my friend = derjenige, welcher
gekommen ist, ist nicht mein Freund.

(Instead of derjenige, welcher the one word wer may be
used if no particular person is indicated.   Wer das sagt,
lügt!   Who (or He who) says that, is lying!)

I have seen your house and your father's.   Ich habe Ihr
Haus und das (or dasjenige) Ihres Vaters gesehen.

Note that instead of derjenige, etc., der, die, das,
pl. die, may be used.

derselbe   dieselbe   dasselbe   dieselben

This word means *the same*, and can be used, just like
derjenige, as either an adjective or a pronoun.

Derselbe Mann, the same man.   Derselbe, the same one.

Exercise 58

Diese Handschuhe sind meine, die anderen sind deine.
Lesen Sie immer dieselbe Zeitung?   Mein Haus ist nicht

so groß wie das Ihrige. Ihr Garten ist länger als der unsrige. Ich habe mein Buch und das meines Bruders gelesen. Ich habe sein Auto gesehen, aber nicht das ihrige. Diejenigen, welche zu spät ankommen, müssen hier warten. Wir essen immer in demselben Restaurant. Er hat immer in derselben Straße gewohnt. Wer nicht arbeitet, soll nicht essen. Sie hat meinen Hut gefunden, aber nicht den seinigen.

Exercise 59

These (das) are your books, not mine. His brother is cleverer than hers. My knife is sharper than yours (du *form*). Both aunts live in the same town. He is reading the same book. Those who do not work hard (= industriously) will learn nothing. Their trees are taller than ours. She always buys the same sweets. Our city is bigger than yours. His work is better than his sister's. His house is not so small as his uncle's. Those who work best may go home early.

LESSON XXII

ORDER OF WORDS

It is now worth while revising all that has been said about the order of words in German. You have now had experience of the order actually used, and so will be ready to appreciate general rules in a way you could not before.

Then shrieked the timid and stood still the brave. Here we have two independent clauses joined by *and*. Each could stand alone and make complete sense—*then the timid shrieked* is one statement, and *the brave stood still* is another. Such clauses are called principal or independent clauses.

The timid shrieked because the ship was sinking. Here

the timid shrieked can stand alone as before and lead to no question. But we cannot read the clause *because the ship was sinking* without knowing that something important has been left out. The second clause, in fact, depends upon the first and is called a dependent or subordinate clause. In the following sentences the principal clause is printed in ordinary type, the subordinate or dependent clause in italics: He said *that he was poor*. The boys *who came this morning* have returned. Go *where he sends you*.

Examining these clauses we find that the words *that he was poor* tell us something. If we ask what he said the answer is *that he was poor*. This clause therefore stands for a thing and in fact does the duty of a noun, and is called a *noun clause*. *Who came this morning* tells us something about the boys, distinguishes these boys from other boys—in fact, it does the work of an adjective, and is called an *adjectival clause*. *Where he sends you* in like manner does the work of an adverb, and is called an *adverbial clause*.

Taking up the principal clause first, we find that, with two important exceptions, the order of words in German is the same as in English *if the sentence begins with the subject*. The two exceptions are:

1. The Past Participle, the Infinitive, and the Separable Prefix are always placed at the end of the clause, and if there be both a Past Participle and an Infinitive, the Infinitive goes to the end and the Past Participle takes the place second from the end. Ich habe das Buch gekauft = I have bought the book; ich werde das Buch kaufen = I shall buy the book; ich kam nach Haus zurück = I came back home; ich werde geliebt werden = I shall be loved.

2. The second exception is of the utmost importance to us, because we are very liable to make mistakes by carrying our English custom into German. In English

we often put an adverb between the subject and the predicate—in fact, the very words we have just used illustrate this: we *often* put, etc. Now, this is never done in German. *We often put*, etc., must read wir setzen oft, etc. No word connected with the predicate can ever come between the subject and the personal verb. There are a few conjunctions which may be placed between the subject and the personal verb; the most usual of these are:

aber, but	nämlich, namely	jedoch, yet, still,
also, so, thus	indessen, whilst, however	however

as:

> Der König aber schlug ihn tot. But the king struck him dead.

You must be continually on your guard against putting in *adverbs* between the subject and its verb.

If for any reason the subject does not begin the clause, a peculiar change called *inversion* takes place, by which the subject is put *after* its personal verb. In English we might say, *The soldier fortunately was present*. This must be translated either: (1) Der Soldat war glücklicherweise zugegen, or (2) Glücklicherweise war der Soldat zugegen.

There are a few little words so insignificant that they may come before the subject without causing inversion. These are:

aber, but	entweder, either	und, and
denn, for	oder, or	

So far we have been dealing with the principal clause. In the case of the *subordinate clause* the essential point is that the verb is placed at the end:

> Der Junge ging ins Bett, weil er krank war. The boy went to bed because he was ill.
> Die Jungen, die heute morgen kamen, sind im Garten. The boys who came this morning are in the garden.
> Gehen Sie, wohin er Sie schickt. Go where he sends you.

In subordinate clauses the Separable Prefix joins up with its verb:

Bevor er ausging, before he went out.

If two infinitives stand at the end, the auxiliaries haben, sein or werden will precede the infinitives instead of following:

Da wir ihn haben finden können, as we have been able to find him.

In all sorts of clauses the following general principles are true:

1. Certain verbs govern two cases, one of which is the accusative, and the other may be either the genitive or the dative. The general rule of order in such cases is that of two nouns the dative comes before the accusative, the genitive after.

Sie werden den König eines Unrechts anklagen. They will accuse the king of an injustice.
Schicken Sie dem Wirte die Briefe. Send the letters to the inn-keeper.

2. A personal pronoun, which is the object (whether direct or indirect) of the verb, generally comes before any noun or adverb in the clause.

Er hat ihnen endlich die Briefe geschickt. He has at last sent them the letters.

3. If there are several adverbs, they are usually arranged in the following order: (1) adverbs of *time*, (2) adverbs of *place*, (3) adverbs of *manner*.

Er hat es zuletzt gut getan. He has done it well at last.
Wir haben morgens im Hause schwer gearbeitet. We worked hard at home in the morning.

Vocabulary

der Strand, beach
der Kieselstein, pebble
der Sand, sand
die Garnele, shrimp

zurückkehren, to return
die Promenade, promenade
das Segel, sail
das Netz, net

der Felsen, rock
die Klippen, cliffs
der Leuchtturm, lighthouse
der Krebs, crab
der Dampfer, steamer
das Segelschiff, sailing-boat
das Fischerboot, fishing-boat
die Pension, boarding-house
das Hotel (—s, —s), hotel
der Liegestuhl, deck-chair
die Hütte, hut
die Strandkabine, bathing-hut
der Badende, bather
die Ferien(pl.) holiday(s)
die Kapelle, orchestra, band
der Sonnenhut, sun-hat
die Welle, wave
*anziehen, to put on (clothes)
aufsetzen, to put on (hat)
*ausziehen, to take off (clothes)
*liegen, to lie (down)
*sitzen, to sit, be seated
mieten, to hire
packen, to pack
Fußball spielen, to play football

das Schwimmbad, bathing-pool
der Badeanzug, bathing-costume
das Sonnenbad, sun-bath
die Boje, buoy
der Spaziergang, walk
der Ausflug, outing, excursion
die (See)möwe, seagull
die Sandburg, sand-castle
die Bademütze, bathing-cap
die Sache, thing, article
*schwimmen, to swim
*verbringen, to spend (time)
*ausgeben, to spend (money)
klettern, to climb
tauchen, to dive
retten, to rescue
*ertrinken, to be drowned
viel Spaß haben, to have a good time
Golf spielen, to play golf
Cricket spielen, to play cricket
der Spaß, joke

die Südküste (Ost-, Nord-, West-), South, East, North, West Coast

Exercise 60

Letzten Sommer verbrachten wir unsere Sommerferien an der Nordküste Deutschlands. Wir packten unsere Koffer und fuhren am 28. August nach Swinemünde. Das Wetter war prachtvoll während des ganzen Monats, den wir dort verbrachten. Wir wohnten in einem großen Hotel, das neben dem Strand war.

Jeden Morgen standen wir früh auf. Nach dem Frühstück gingen wir zum Strand hinunter. Wir brachten unsere Badeanzüge mit, und wenn das Wetter warm war, zogen wir unsere Badeanzüge an, setzten wir unsere Bademützen auf, und schwammen in der See. Ich kann nicht wie (like) ein Fisch schwimmen, doch (yet) schwimme ich sehr gern. Einige kleine Kinder, deren Eltern (parents) in Liegestühlen saßen, machten Sandburgen. Andere spielten Fußball oder suchten Garnelen

und Krebse mit ihren Netzen.   Nach dem Baden lagen
wir auf dem warmen Sand und nahmen ein Sonnenbad.
Bald wurden wir sehr braun, fast wie Neger (Negroes).
Eines Tages sahen wir einen Jungen in der See.   Er
konnte nicht sehr gut schwimmen.   Ein Fischer hat ihn
vom Ertrinken gerettet.

Manchmal machten wir einen Ausflug auf einem
Fischerboot.   Das war sehr schön, und wir hatten viel
Spaß.   Wir tauchten von dem Boot in die See.   Es
war sehr schön, wenn die Wellen groß waren.   Oft
kletterten wir die Klippen hinauf, oder machten einen
Spaziergang den Strand entlang.[1]

Mein Vater hatte eine Strandkabine gemietet, und so
konnten wir nachmittags Kaffee am Strand trinken.
Mein Vater spielte oft Golf auf dem schönen Golfplatz.
Wir waren sehr traurig, als wir nach Hause zurückkehren
mußten.

Exercise 61

I want to leave for Stuttgart tomorrow morning.   In
the autumn we must pick the apples and plough the
fields.   Where is the basket into which I put the apples?
At Christmas we have four days' holiday.   We must not
smoke here, for it is forbidden.   The child whose parents
are dead is very clever.   I cannot read this letter because it is so badly written.   Therefore you must show
me the letter you wrote this morning.   Yesterday it
rained as I was coming up the street.   The man to whom
I was talking yesterday is the major.   Before you go out
show me the newspaper you bought this morning.   He
went out yesterday evening although he was ill.   As it
was so late he went immediately to bed.   Whilst he was
putting on his coat he heard somebody at the door.

[1] Entlang usually follows the noun in the accusative: *along
the beach.*

LESSON XXIII

PASSIVE VOICE

The Imperfect of werden is very easy:

Imperfect of werden

Singular	Plural
1. ich wurde	wir wurden
2. du wurdest	{ Sie wurden { ihr wurdet
3. er wurde	sie wurden

We can use werden with the Past Participle as well as with the Infinitive, but then it has quite a different meaning.

Ich werde lieben = I shall love.
Ich werde geliebt = I am loved.

Werden and the Infinitive make the Future tense; werden and the Past Participle make what is called the Passive voice. The Passive indicates that the subject of the verb does not act, but is rather acted upon. It indicates how the subject is affected by the action of others upon it.

The four commonest tenses of the Passive are: the Present, *I am loved*; the Imperfect, *I was loved*; the Perfect, *I have been loved*; and the Pluperfect, *I had been loved*.

Present: ich werde geliebt.
Imperfect: ich wurde geliebt.

To make the two Perfect tenses we require the Past Participle of werden. This Past Participle is geworden.

Note that this Past Participle has no ge before it when it is used to form the Passive of another verb.

Ich bin geworden means "I have become".
Ich war geworden means "I had become".

So if we put in the Past Participle of lieben we get:

> Ich bin geliebt worden, meaning "I have become loved"
> or, more simply, "I have been loved".
> Ich war geliebt worden, means "I had become loved" or
> "I had been loved".

Sometimes the Past Participle is used like an adjective, and when this is done there is apt to be some confusion with the Passive. If we find a soldier lying dead with a bullet hole in his head we may say: Er ist getötet = he is killed. Here there is no action, therefore no Passive voice. Er wird getötet is the Passive form, and implies that he is being killed: that the killing is going on. When you are in doubt whether a Participle is to be used as a Passive or not, ask yourself whether you can put this action into the progressive form. Bestrafen = to punish. *I am punished.* Is the punishing going on? Yes; then ich werde bestraft. No; then ich bin bestraft. The following examples will help to make this point clear.

> I shall punish. Ich werde bestrafen.
> The soldiers are being rescued. Die Soldaten werden
> gerettet.
> The soldiers were rescued (*i.e.* were in the state of now being
> safe). Die Soldaten waren gerettet.
> They had been rescued. Sie waren gerettet worden.
> I have been punished. Ich bin bestraft worden.
> She is asked. Sie wird gefragt.

When *by* is used with the Passive it is always rendered von to denote the *agent*, durch to denote the *instrument*:

> Der Knabe wird *von* seinem Vater bestraft. The boy is
> punished by his father.
> Der Soldat wurde *durch* einen Pfeil getötet. The soldier
> was killed by an arrow.

Exercise 62

Put in the proper form of sein or werden (to form either Passive or Future) according to the meaning:

Dieser Briefkasten — dreimal am Tage (a day) vom Briefträger geleert (emptied). Dieser Brief — gestern von meiner Stenotypistin geschrieben. — der Brief schon geschrieben? Ich — meinen Freund in Bonn besuchen. Das Telegramm — gestern geschickt. Als wir ankamen, — die Tür schon geschlossen. Das Haus — schon gebaut worden. Dieses Kleid — letztes Jahr vom Schneider gemacht.

Exercise 63

I have been asked by my brother to[1] go to Berlin. These apples were picked yesterday by the baker's children. When (wann) will these letters be written? The child has been punished. This newspaper is read every day by thousands of (Tausenden von) men and women. Has the car already been repaired? Have you been seen by anyone? The letter-box is now being cleared (emptied) by the postman. This dress will be made by the tailor. When was this book written?

LESSON XXIV

GOVERNMENT OF VERBS

I. Verbs taking the Dative

As we have seen before, there are certain verbs which sometimes require *to* in English when the Dative without preposition is required in German. Such verbs take two objects, a direct and an indirect, this preceding the direct if both are nouns, and following if both are pronouns. If one is a pronoun and the other a noun, the pronoun comes first. Such are:

sich nähern, to approach
*geben, to give
schenken, to present

*(an)bieten, to offer
widmen, to dedicate, devote
*schreiben, to write[2]

---

[1] Zu.   Do not forget that the infinitive goes to the end.
[2] Also an + Acc. before noun.

reichen, to pass
schicken, to send
erwidern, to reply
zeigen, to show
*beschreiben, to describe
*befehlen, to order
erlauben ⎫
gestatten ⎭ to allow

sagen, to tell[1]
erzählen, to relate, tell
*leihen, to lend
*vorlesen, to read (aloud) to
verweigern ⎫
*abschlagen ⎭ to refuse
vertrauen, to trust
anvertrauen, to entrust

Examples:

Ich näherte mich dem Löwen.   I drew near to the lion.
Er vertraute seinem Bruder das Kind an.   He entrusted the child to his brother.
Wir schlugen es ihm ab.   We refused it him.

The following govern the Dative, where the reason is not so apparent to the English student:

danken, to thank
antworten, to answer (person)
begegnen, to meet
gehorchen, to obey
*geschehen, to happen
*helfen, to help
passen, to fit

dienen, to serve
folgen, to follow
*gefallen, to please
gehören, to belong
glauben, to believe (person)
nützen, to be of use
schmeicheln, to flatter

2. Verbs governing the Genitive

The Genitive noun *follows* the Accusative.

sich bedienen, to use
sich schämen,[3] to be ashamed of
berauben, to rob of
versichern, to assure of

sich erinnern,[2] to remember
anklagen, to accuse of
überzeugen, to convince of

3. Verbs followed by the Nominative

*bleiben, to remain
*heißen, to be called

*sein, to be
*werden, to become

4. Verbs taking a different Preposition

All the following verbs taking a preposition different from that in English take the Accusative, except those marked with a dagger (†), and these require the Dative.

---

[1] To say to = sagen zu.
[2] Also takes an + Acc.
[3] Also takes über + Acc.

(a) An:

adressieren, to address (*message*)
*denken, to think of
*sterben, to die of (*illness*) (†)
*sich wenden, to apply to
zweifeln, to doubt (†)

glauben, to believe
sich lehnen, to lean against
erinnern, to remind of
sich erinnern, to remember
*teilnehmen, to take part in (†)

(b) Auf:

*achtgeben, to pay attention to
antworten, to answer (*thing*)
zählen, to count on

warten, to wait for
*sich verlassen, to rely on
sich freuen, to look forward to

(c) Aus:

*werden, to become (†)
*bestehen, to consist of (†)

übersetzen, to translate
   from (†)
machen, to make from (†)

(d) Bei:

*bleiben, to stay with (†)

wohnen, to live with (†)

(e) Nach:

fragen, to ask for (†)
zielen, to aim at (†)

schicken, to send for (†)
sich sehnen, to long for (†)

(f) Uber:

sich ärgern, to be annoyed at
erstaunen, to be surprised at
sich wundern, to wonder at
sich freuen, to rejoice at
sich schämen, to be ashamed of

lachen, to laugh at[1]
spotten, to make fun of
erröten, to blush at
sich aufregen, to get excited at

(g) Um:

spielen, to play for
*bitten, to ask for

kämpfen, to struggle for

(h) Vor:

sich fürchten,[2] to be afraid of (†)
zittern, to tremble with (†)

warnen, to warn of (†)
schützen, to protect from (†)

Note also: vor Freude tanzen, to dance for joy
          vor Hunger sterben, to die of hunger

[1] But: I laugh at him. Ich lache ihn aus.
[2] I fear that . . . = ich fürchte, daß . . .

Exercise 64

Ich dankte ihm für seinen Brief. Er starb an Gicht (gout). Er ärgerte sich über meine Antwort. Ich fragte nach dem Preis (price) der Äpfel. Er hat dieses Buch aus dem Deutschen übersetzt, während er bei seiner Tante wohnte. Er befahl dem Manne, auf den Zug zu warten. Das Mädchen errötete über diese Antwort. Ich vertraue Ihnen diese Arbeit an. Wem gehört das Haus mit dem roten Dach? Erlauben Sie mir, Ihnen zu helfen. Ich las meiner Mutter den Brief vor. Beschreiben Sie mir die Stadt, in der Sie wohnen. Erinnern Sie sich an den Tag, wo[1] wir dem Manne begegneten? Was ist aus Ihrem Bruder geworden? Der Junge lehnte sich an die Wand. Folgen Sie mir, bitte! Gefällt es Ihnen hier in England? Das englische Wetter gefällt mir nicht. Sie können sich auf ihn verlassen. Wann haben Sie Ihrer Schwester diese Armbanduhr geschenkt? Die anderen lachten und spotteten über den armen Jungen. Das kleine Mädchen fürchtete sich vor der großen Kuh. Der arme Mann bat mich um Geld (money). Wir zitterten vor Kälte (cold).

Exercise 65

The girls and boys danced for joy. My nephew has become a sailor. I was surprised at his letter. Whom are you thinking of? Ask (for) the price of the coat in the shop-window. Pass the sugar to your brother, please. Did you like the film yesterday evening? I do not believe her. Have you not sent for the doctor? I fear that we shall have bad weather tomorrow. I allowed the children to play in the garden. We told the policeman the whole story (die Geschichte). He asked me for money, but I refused it him. I do not remember the girl. He got excited at my answer, and ordered me to show him the book. He leaned against the door and

[1] *When* after a noun of time = wo.

would not allow me to go out.   Are you afraid of lions?
There is the man whom we met at the "Red Lion".

LESSON XXV

THE ENGLISH PRESENT PARTICIPLE

The English Present Participle of the verb (*i.e.* the
part ending in *-ing*) is a fruitful source of difficulty to
the English student of German.   Here is a list of the
main points to be noticed:

1. The German Present Participle in -end is used as an
adjective before the noun (rarely can it be used after
it), and it may be used adverbially or to form a noun
which in English would end in *-er*:

> Der sterbende Mann,[1] the dying man.
> Sie hat eine auffallend musikalische Stimme.   She has a
>   strikingly musical voice.
> Der Reisende,[2] der Badende, the traveller, the bather.

2. After the verb bleiben, *to remain*, and those mentioned in the next lesson, under the Infinitive, section
1 (*c*), the English Present Participle is rendered by the
simple Infinitive:

> Er blieb sitzen.   He remained sitting.
> Ich sah ihn spielen.   I saw him playing.

3. When the English Present Participle is a noun the
simple Infinitive is used in German:

> Das Rauchen ist hier verboten.   Smoking is forbidden here.
> Er ist des Wartens müde.   He is tired of waiting.

---

[1] But we cannot say: Der Mann ist sterbend.   We can say:
Das Mädchen ist reizend, *the girl is charming*, because reizend is
purely adjectival, whereas sterbend is verbal in force.

[2] Such nouns, and those formed from adjectives or Past
Participles, are declined as though they were adjectives followed
by a noun.

(Note the position of müde: adjectives in German frequently come at the end like this.)

4. In most other cases it is best to turn the Present Participle into a clause, co-ordinate with und, subordinate or relative, according to the meaning. Note the following:

> He sat smoking on a chair = he sat on a chair and smoked.
> The girl wearing the green dress = the girl who wears the green dress.
> On opening the window = when I opened.
> Before going out = before I went out.
> Knowing he was ill = as I knew he was ill.
> "Yes," he said, putting on his coat = whilst he put on his coat.

5. After kommen, *to come*, the Germans have a curious use of the Past Participle instead of the Present Participle to denote the mode of coming:

> Er kam gehüpft, gelaufen, gesprungen, gekrochen, he came hopping, running, jumping, crawling, etc.

Exercise 66

Bevor er ins Bett ging, schrieb er einen Brief. Nachdem er die Zeitung gelesen hatte, ging er aus. Indem er seinen Mantel anzog und seinen Hut aufsetzte, lief er aus dem Zimmer. Das Baden ist hier verboten. Er saß im Garten und rauchte eine Pfeife. Wer ist das Mädchen, das den grünen Hut trägt? Wir hörten unsere Kusine singen. Er blieb an der Tür stehen. Da ich wußte (knew),[1] daß er zu Hause war, telefonierte ich mit ihm. Als ich zum Fenster hinaussah, sah ich das Auto unseres Arztes vorbeifahren. Er sah sie Tennis spielen. Er rauchte, während er sich rasierte. Das kleine Mädchen kam gelaufen und sprach zu uns. Ich stand auf, als ich den Mann hereinkommen sah, aber meine Schwester blieb sitzen.

[1] *Wissen, *to know* through the brain (*facts*).
*Kennen, *to know* by sight, hearing, touch, smell, taste.

Exercise 67

Seeing the letter on the table I read it. "Are you ready?" he asked, putting on his coat. He stood near the door, reading a newspaper. The man was working and his wife was playing the piano. I asked him to sit[1] down, but he remained standing. On opening the drawer we found a letter from him. Who is the man riding the big black horse? We found them weeping. Before going out he 'phoned his brother. Knowing it was late we decided not to visit our uncle. After seeing the advertisement in the paper he 'phoned his sister. The dying sailor asked for water. The man is dying. Going along the street I met my dentist. I used to know this doctor. He knows nothing.

LESSON XXVI

VERBS WITH SEIN—THE INFINITIVE

Up till now we have always used the verb haben to make the Perfect or Pluperfect of a verb, as in ich habe es getan = I have done it. But there are a good many verbs that require the verb sein instead of the verb haben. In English we usually say *I have come*, but in German it must be *I am come*, ich bin gekommen.

Lists are sometimes given of verbs that take sein and those that take haben, but these are very tiresome to learn, and it is better if we can hit upon any way of discovering *from the meaning* whether a verb should have haben or sein. It may be accepted as a rule that *all* verbs having a direct object must use haben. Of other verbs, the sein class may be detected by applying the following test: Is the action of the verb followed by a

---

[1] *To sit down* (take one's seat), sich setzen.
  To sit, be sitting, be seated, *sitzen.

corresponding state? If it is, then use sein; if it is not, use haben. The question may be best put—If I have done so-and-so, am I so-and-so?

For example: If I have come, am I come? The answer is clearly *yes*; so we use sein. If I have died, am I dead? Again *yes*; so we use sein. Er ist gestorben = he has died. If I have fought, am I fought? The answer is *no*; so we write er hat gekämpft.

Some of the commonest verbs of the sein class are:

*bleiben, to remain, stay	reisen, to travel
eilen, to hurry	*gelingen, to succeed
*fliegen, to fly	*kommen, to come
*fallen, to fall	*steigen, to mount
*sein, to be	*werden, to become
*sinken, to sink	*wachsen, to grow
*gehen, to go	wandern, to wander

The Infinitive

1. The Infinitive *without* zu is used after

    (*a*) the verb werden,
    (*b*) the modal auxiliaries (müssen, können, etc.),
    (*c*) the following verbs:

*helfen, to help	fühlen, to feel
hören, to hear	lehren, to teach
*lassen, to cause	lernen, to learn
*sehen, to see	

We have already seen this in the case of werden and the Modal Auxiliaries. Here are examples of the others:

Ich sah sie spielen.	I saw her *playing*.
Sie lehrten mich singen.	They taught me to sing.
Ich lernte dort schwimmen.	I learnt to swim there.

The zu is also omitted in certain expressions:

Er geht schwimmen.	He is going swimming.
Er tut nichts als schlafen.	He does nothing but sleep.

2. In other cases zu is used before the Infinitive. Remember that zu comes between the Separable Prefix and the Infinitive, forming one word, but in other cases forms two words:

Er bat mich, ihn zu begleiten. He asked me to accompany him.

Ich wünschte auszugehen. I desired to go out.

Ich versprach, früh nach Hause zu kommen. I promised to come home early.

Er befahl mir, nach Berlin zu reisen. He ordered me to go to Berlin.

Wir beschlossen in Bonn zu übernachten. We decided to stay the night in Bonn.

The verb lassen

The verb lassen mentioned in Section 1 above is very important. It means *to have something done, to cause something to be done, to get something done.* Like the Modal Auxiliaries, the Infinitive instead of the Past Participle is used after another Infinitive. Note these examples:

Ich lasse mir die Haare schneiden. I have (am having) my hair cut.

Ich ließ mir die Haare schneiden. I had my hair cut.

Ich habe mir die Haare schneiden lassen. I have had my hair cut.

Ich werde mir die Haare schneiden lassen. I shall have my hair cut.

Ich beschloß, mir die Haare schneiden zu lassen. I decided to have my hair cut.

Note 1. The English *Past Participle* in such cases is in German the *Infinitive.* *Cut* (Past Participle) becomes in German *to cut.* The exact meaning is: *I cause to cut.*

Note 2. In talking of parts of the *body* or *dress*, unless any misunderstanding might arise, the definite article is used instead of the possessive adjective (*my*, *his*, etc.). Possession is indicated by the Dative of the noun or pronoun:

Ich ließ mir die Haare schneiden. I had my hair cut.

This is true of constructions other than with lassen:

Ich trat dem Manne auf den Fuß. I trod on the man's foot (*literally:* I trod to the man on the foot).

Ich wusch mir die Hände. I washed my hands.

But: Seine Hände waren furchtbar schmutzig. His hands were terribly dirty. (If die were used, possession would be vague and the sentence would be ridiculous.)

Exercise 68

Ich gehe heute nachmittag mit meinem Freund schwimmen. Hast du versprochen, ihm ein Buch zu schicken? Mein Onkel lehrte mich Klavier spielen. Ich lasse mir die Haare schneiden. Ich habe mir ein neues Haus bauen lassen. Wo haben Sie Golf spielen gelernt? Helfen Sie mir einsteigen! Müssen Sie jetzt nach Hause gehen? Wir werden uns in Paris neue Kleider machen lassen. Er beschloß, mit dem Auto nach Köln zu fahren. Ich beschloß, mir die Haare schneiden zu lassen. Mein Vater hat mir versprochen, mich vom Bahnhof abzuholen. Wünschen Sie morgen abzufahren? Ich befahl dem Kellner, mir eine Flasche Wein zu bringen. Ich habe mir eine Flasche Wein bringen lassen. Wir sahen ihn im Walde reiten. Waschen Sie ihm die Hände! Hast du dir die Hände gewaschen? Ich habe ihm die Hände gewaschen. Der Friseur (barber) hat dem Manne die Haare geschnitten. Schneiden Sie mir bitte die Haare nicht zu kurz! Hast du dir die Fingernägel (finger-nails) lackiert (painted) und die Augenbrauen rasiert (shaved = plucked)? Ich lasse mir die Schuhe putzen (clean). Ist er nach Hause gegangen? Sie sind noch nicht angekommen. Mein Bruder ist gestern nach Amsterdam geflogen.

Exercise 69

I heard you singing in the garden. Who taught you to play the piano? Shall I buy you a few cigarettes when I am in the town? We have hurried to the station to meet you. Have you travelled to Russia? The trees in your garden have grown very tall. I had the grass of the lawn cut yesterday. I shall have a new suit made next week. We have often wandered over these fields. Have you stayed at home all day? Can you get this wheel repaired for me? I have had a glass of wine brought for you. Shall I have these things sent (zuschicken) to you? I have decided to have my hair waved (ondulieren). Will you teach me to dive? We promised to send them a letter every week. He asked her to write to him. Have you ordered the waiter to bring some more bread? No, I have ordered[1] some cigarettes. Do you wish to listen to the wireless?

LESSON XXVII

THE SUBJUNCTIVE

I. The Formation of the Subjunctive

The Present Tense

In learning the Subjunctive forms of the verbs the student must remember the "Subjunctive e". All the endings have e, as the following examples will show, and in the Present Tense this e is added in all cases to the stem of the verb, *i.e.* that part left after taking off -(e)n:

haben	lieben	müssen
hab-e	lieb-e	müss-e
hab-est	lieb-est	müss-est
hab-e	lieb-e	müss-e
hab-en	lieb-en	müss-en
hab-et	lieb-et	müss-et
hab-en	lieb-en	müss-en

The one exception to this is the verb sein:

sei	seien
seiest	seiet
sei	seien

You will note the ich sei and er sei have no e.

The Imperfect Tense

In the case of *Weak* Verbs there is nothing to learn, as their Imperfect Tense is exactly the same as the In-dicative.

[1] *To order* something, bestellen. *To order* a person to do something, *befehlen.

Strong Verbs form the Imperfect Subjunctive by adding the e endings given above to the stem of the Imperfect Indicative, which is modified when possible.

Infinitive	sein	haben	müssen	singen
Imperfect Ind.	war	hatte	mußte	sang
Imperfect Subj.	wäre	hätte	müßte	sänge

2. Use of the Subjunctive

One of the most important uses of the Subjunctive is in *Indirect* or *Reported Speech*. Notice the following:

Direct Speech: He said: "I *am* ill."
Indirect Speech: He said he *was* ill.

In English the Present Tense (*am*) becomes Past Tense (*was*) in Indirect Speech. In German the Present Tense of Direct Speech should correctly become the Present Subjunctive, but many Germans use the Imperfect Subjunctive, especially in conversation:

Direct Speech: Er sagte: "Ich bin krank."
Indirect Speech: Er sagte, daß er krank sei (or wäre).

The daß in Indirect Speech may be omitted. Notice the word order:

Er sagte, er sei (or wäre) krank.

The Present Subjunctive is *not* used if it has the same form as the Present Indicative. The Imperfect Subjunctive must be used in such a case. Let us compare the Present Subjunctive and Present Indicative of the verb haben:

Pres. Subj.	*Pres. Ind.*
ich habe	habe
habest	hast
habe	hat
wir haben	haben
habet	habt
sie haben	haben

Thus those forms which are the same in both moods are the ich, wir and sie forms, and they must be replaced by hätte, hätten. As, however, the Imperfect Subjunctive may be used in all cases, and usually is in conversational style, the student is advised to *keep to the Imperfect Subjunctive in Reported Speech*, until his command of the language is more complete.

If the tense of the actual words is *Past* in English, then the student should use the *Pluperfect* (although more correctly the Perfect, except when this is the same as the Perfect Indicative in form):

Direct: The policeman said: "I found the book."
Indirect: The policeman said he (had) found the book.

In German:

Direct: Der Schutzmann sagte: "Ich habe das Buch gefunden."
Indirect: Der Schutzmann sagte, daß er das Buch gefunden hätte (sagte, er hätte das Buch gefunden).

General Rule for the Subjunctive in Indirect Speech

After a verb (in the Past Tense) of *saying, declaring, believing, asking,*[1] *answering, reporting, fearing, thinking, relating, suspecting, surmising,* etc., the Subjunctive must be used in the following clause as explained above.

Another use of the Subjunctive is the 3rd Person Imperative form (see also p. 89):

Er gehe nach Hause!
or: Er soll nach Hause gehen. } Let him go home.
or: Laßt ihn nach Hause gehen!

Notice also the exclamatory wish:

Es lebe der König! } Long live the King!
Hoch lebe der König!

Vocabulary

der Salon, drawing-room	das Wohnzimmer, living-room
der Schlüssel, key	die Elektrizität, electricity

[1] Fragen, *to ask*, takes ob, *whether, if*, which, unlike daß, may never be omitted.

der Stock (das Stockwerk), storey, floor
der Aufzug, lift
der Heizkörper, radiator
die Zentralheizung, central heating
der Ofen, German stove[1]
der Vorhang, curtain
der Wecker, alarm-clock
der Kleiderständer, coat-rack
der Schirmständer, umbrella-stand
der Rollvorhang, blind
*hinaufgehen, to go up
*hinunterlaufen, to run down
anknipsen, to switch on
aufwachen, to wake up
modern,[2] modern, up-to-date
schuldig, owing
das Gas, gas
das Studierzimmer, study
die Garage, garage
das Schlafzimmer, bedroom
das Badezimmer, bathroom
die Treppe, stairs
der Schornstein, chimney

das Feuer, fire
der Boden, floor
der Teppich, carpet
der Spiegel, mirror
der Kamin, mantelpiece, English fireplace
*bekommen } to get, obtain,
kriegen } receive
*schließen, to lock
*herunterlassen, to let down
hängen, to hang
*heraufziehen, to pull up
beleuchtet, lighted
klingeln (nach), to ring (for)
bedecken, to cover
sich wärmen, to warm oneself
ausmachen, to put out
wecken, to wake (someone)
*hinauffahren, to go up (in a lift)
die Mark (no pl.), mark
sicher, certain(ly)
die Nummer, number
bitte sehr! not at all!
was für, what sort of
*vergessen, to forget

Exercise 70

Chauffeur, fahren Sie zu einem modernen, aber billigen Hotel! Ich will in dieser Stadt einige Wochen verbringen. Hier ist ein gutes Hotel, mein Herr: der Riesenfürstenhof. Gut! Ich steige hier aus. Wieviel bin ich Ihnen schuldig? Drei Mark fünfzig? (Gibt ihm ein Trinkgeld.) Danke schön, mein Herr! Bitte sehr! Kann ich ein Zimmer für einige Nächte bekommen? Ja, sicher! Was für eines? Ich will nicht zu viel ausgeben.

Der Mann sagte, er hätte einige schöne Zimmer, die ganz ruhig und hell beleuchtet wären. Ich antwortete, daß ich sie sehen möchte. Er sagte, ich könnte mit dem Aufzug hinauffahren: Nummer 15. Ich fragte, wo der Aufzug wäre. Er erwiderte, daß er in der Ecke wäre. Ich fragte den Liftboy, ob das Hotel Zentralheizung

---

[1] A stove for heating purposes which replaces the English open fireplace.   [2] Pron. mo-dern'.

hätte. "Ja, sicher!" antwortete er. Er fragte, zu welchem Zimmer ich ginge. Ich sagte, daß ich dort einige Tage verbringen würde. Ich fragte, ob das Hotel eine Garage hätte. Ob das Hotel in allen Zimmern durch Elektrizität beleuchtet wäre. Er sagte mir, daß ein Badezimmer neben meinem Zimmer wäre, und daß Zentralheizung in allen Zimmern wäre.

Ich klingelte nach dem Portier. Ich fragte ihn, ob er mich um 5 Uhr wecken würde. Er antwortete, daß er es nicht vergessen würde. Ich zog den Rollvorhang herauf und sah auf die Straße hinunter.

Exercise 71

The driver said he was ready. I asked him if he knew (wissen or kennen?) where the Hotel Bismarck was. He said he had never seen it. I asked the policeman whether the post office was in this street. She said he was coming on Monday. The girl said she had seen his car in the garage. The man told me she had gone by air to England. I replied that I had missed the train. She asked me if I would like to play with them. Long live our friend from Germany!

LESSON XXVIII

THE CONDITIONAL SENTENCE

The so-called Conditional tense or mood is formed with the Imperfect Subjunctive of werden + the Infinitive.

ich würde gehen	I should[1] go
du würdest gehen	you would[2] go

---

[1] The English *should* also means *ought to:* we shall deal with this later in this lesson.

[2] The English *would* also means *wanted to* and *used to:*

He would not answer. Er wollte nicht antworten.

He would often go out in the evenings. Er ging oft abends aus (oft ging er abends aus).

er würde gehen	he would go
wir würden gehen	we should go
ihr würdet gehen	you would go
sie würden gehen	they would go
Sie würden gehen	you would go

The above tense, as we prefer to call it, is used when an *if* is expressed or understood, and to translate *should* or *would* in Indirect Speech:

> Ich würde das Haus kaufen, wenn es billiger wäre. I should buy the house if it were cheaper.
>
> Er sagte, daß sie kommen würde. He said she would be coming.

The *If* Clause

As will be seen above, wenn, *if*, is followed by the Imperfect Subjunctive to express a hypothesis or condition impossible or unlikely to be fulfilled.

> Wenn ich das Geld hätte. If I had the money.
> Wenn er nach Hause käme. If he came (were to come) home.

The wenn, like the *if* in English, may be omitted:

> Hätte ich das Geld. Had I the money (= if I had).

The würde clause may be replaced by the Imperfect Subjunctive, while the Pluperfect Subjunctive is much to be preferred to the Second or Perfect Conditional. This subjunctive construction in both Simple and Second Conditional must be used in the case of the Modal Auxiliaries, as set out on page 137. Consider the following examples:

1. SIMPLE CONDITIONAL: *If he were here I would show it to him* may be translated:

> (i) Wenn er hier wäre, würde ich es ihm zeigen, or
> (ii) Wäre er hier, zeigte ich es ihm, or
> (iii) Wenn er hier wäre, zeigte ich es ihm, or
> (iv) Wäre er hier, würde ich es ihm zeigen.

Or the second clause may be put first. Of the above perhaps it is best for the student to keep to the first.

2. SECOND CONDITIONAL: *If he had been here I would have shown it to him* may be translated:

(i) Wenn er hier gewesen wäre (Wäre er hier gewesen)» hätte ich es ihm gezeigt.
(ii) Wenn er hier gewesen wäre (Wäre er hier gewesen), würde ich es ihm gezeigt haben.

Of these two the student had better keep to the former, that being the more usual.

The Modal Auxiliaries

We have said before that the Imperfect Subjunctive of the modal auxiliaries is used instead of the Simple Conditional with würde, and the Pluperfect Subjunctive instead of the Second Conditional:

Simple Conditional:

Ich könnte nicht gehen.   I could not (should not be able to) go.
Ich müßte Deutsch lernen.   I should have to learn German.
Ich möchte diesen Film sehen.   I should like to see this film.
Ich sollte nach Hause gehen.   I should (ought to) go home.

Second Conditional:

Ich hätte nicht gehen können.   I could not have gone (should not have been able to go).
Ich hätte Deutsch lernen müssen.   I should have had to learn German.
Ich hätte gerne diesen Film gesehen.   I should have liked to see this film (preferable to the construction with mögen).
Ich hätte nach Hause gehen sollen.   I should (ought to) have gone home.

Als ob, als wenn, as though, as if

If followed by a Past tense als ob and als wenn are followed by a *past subjunctive*:

Er sieht aus, als ob er ein Gespenst gesehen hätte.   He looks as though he had seen a ghost.

Exercise 72

If you had the money would you like to go to the United States?   If I were you I should go home at once (gleich). Had my friend been at home I should have spent the night with him. She would have missed the train if she had not gone to the station by taxi. I should have telephoned you had I not been able to come. I told them I would help them if I could. I should have liked to go with you to the theatre, but I was terribly busy. If the lift had been in order I should not have fallen (fallen) down the stairs. I asked him how much I owed him. He asked me if I was getting out there. I asked him if he could switch on the light. He asked me if I desired to go up by the lift. I told him I got a letter from her every week. The driver asked me to what sort of hotel I would like to go. I told him I had come up the stairs. The liftboy said he put an alarm-clock on the mantelpiece of my room. The girl looked as though she had spent several weeks by the (an der) sea.

LESSON XXIX

REFLEXIVE VERBS

(i) When the action of a verb is reflected back to the subject the Reflexive Pronoun must be used, even after a preposition. The Reflexive Pronoun is Accusative if the direct object and Dative if indirect.

Accusative

ich wasche mich, I wash myself
*du wäschst dich, you wash yourself
er wäscht sich, he washes himself
sie wäscht sich, she washes herself
wir waschen uns, we wash ourselves
ihr wascht euch, you wash yourselves
sie waschen sich, they wash themselves
Sie waschen sich, you wash yourself (yourselves)

* Or: du wäschest.

Imperfect
ich wusch mich, I washed myself

Perfect
Ich habe mich gewaschen, I have washed myself

Dative
ich wasche mir die Hände, I wash my hands, etc.
du wäschst dir   ,,
er wäscht sich   ,,
sie wäscht sich   ,,
wir waschen uns   ,,
ihr wascht euch   ,,
sie waschen sich   ,,
Sie waschen sich   ,,

He looked behind him.	Er blickte hinter sich.
He spoke to himself.	Er sprach vor sich hin.
He has no money on him.	Er hat kein Geld bei sich.

(ii) In English *myself*, *himself*, etc., are frequently used, not reflexively, but to add force to the subject. In such cases selber or selbst must be used in German and placed after the direct object:

He did it himself.   Er tat es selbst.

(iii) In English we commonly use what is sometimes called a neuter verb to express a passive state when the agent is unknown or too unimportant in the mind of the speaker. In such cases the active reflexive verb is often used in German:

Suddenly the door opened.   Plötzlich öffnete sich die Tür.

(iv) Here is a list of verbs which are "neuter" in English and where the German reflexive is easily understood:

sich ändern, to change (= vary)	sich rasieren, to shave
*sich anziehen, to dress	*sich waschen, to wash
*sich ausziehen, to undress	sich regen, to stir, move
sich fühlen, to feel	sich rühren, to move (away)
sich lehnen, to lean	sich umdrehen, to turn round

(v) Here is a list of verbs where the German reflexive is not so apparent:

*sich befinden,[1] to be (found)
sich bemühen, to endeavour
*sich umsehen, to have a look round
sich aufregen, to get excited
sich legen, to lie down
sich irren, to be mistaken
*sich betragen, to behave
sich erkälten, to catch cold
sich freuen, to be glad
sich erinnern,[2] to remember

sich fragen, to wonder
sich setzen, to sit down
sich weigern, to refuse
sich verirren, to lose one's way
sich totlachen, to die of laughing
sich erholen, to recover (health)
*sich unterhalten, to converse
sich beeilen, to hasten, hurry
sich bedienen,[3] to use

(vi) Verbs with the Dative Reflexive Pronoun:

*sich vornehmen, to propose, plan, arrange
*sich wehtun, to hurt oneself

sich vorstellen ⎱ to imagine
sich einbilden ⎰

(vii) The Reflexive Pronoun in the Dative is also often used as (*a*) the Dative of Advantage, and (*b*) to indicate possession where the article is used instead of the possessive adjective in talking of parts of the body or dress (see Lesson XXVI, under: The verb lassen, page 129).

(*a*) Dative of Advantage:

Er ließ sich ein Haus bauen.   He had a house built for himself.
Er kaufte sich ein Radio.   He bought himself a wireless.
Ich sah mir die Schaufenster an.   I had a look at the shopwindows.

(*b*) In speaking of the body or dress:

Er schnitt sich in den Finger.   He cut his finger.
Er brach sich das Genick.   He broke his neck.
Ich ließ mir die Haare schneiden.   I had my hair cut.

Vocabulary

der Wunsch, wish
von mir, of mine
sich erfüllen, to be fulfilled
abgesehen von, apart from
*wiedersehen, to see again

bewundern, to admire
enttäuschen, to disappoint
der Reisemorgen, morning of the departure
*anbrechen, to break, dawn

---

[1] Sich befinden = to be in health *or* be situated.
[2] Sich erinnern takes the Genitive or an with Acc.
[3] Sich bedienen takes the Genitive.

besonders, particularly
so viel, so much
die Schönheit, beauty
eigen, own
die Eisenbahn, railway
endlich, at last
mieten, to hire
das Schiff, ship
der Weg, way
die Sperre, barrier
passieren, to pass
sorgfältig, careful(ly)
prüfen, to examine
der Reisepaß, passport
schützen, to protect
zollpflichtig, dutiable
verneinen, to say no
*vorbeilassen, to allow to pass
der Holzsteg, wooden gangway
gebräunt, sun-tanned
wetterhart, weather-beaten
der Zug, feature
*herumlaufen, to run about
das Gesicht, face
läuten, to ring, tinkle
sich schaukeln, to toss, pitch
der Schaum, foam
der Bug, bow (of ship)
die Einwanderung, immigration
sich's bequem machen, to make oneself comfortable
seefest, a good sailor
*sinken, to sink
der Zollbeamte, Customs officer
der Einwanderungsbeamte, immigration officer

der Wettergott, "clerk of the weather"
herabstrahlen, to shine down
die (Bahn)fahrt, (railway) journey
das Deck, deck
bekannt, acquainted
die Reise, journey
vertraut, familiar
bequem, comfortable
seekrank, seasick
laut, loud
ohrenbetäubend, deafening
das Sirenengeheul, blast of the siren
anzeigen, to indicate
der Hafen, harbour
offen, open
gekräuselt, ruffled
malerisch, picturesque
der Eindruck, impression
immer ferner, further and further
rücken, to move
an etwas (Dat.) *vorbeifahren, to go past something
die Boje, buoy
der Westen, the west
*einfahren, to enter (vehicle)
aufspritzen, to splash up
plaudern, to converse, chat
einander, one another
zu, to, for
der Inhalt, contents
untersuchen, to overhaul
neugeboren,[1] new-born
Gott sei Dank! Thank Heaven!

Exercise 73

Eine Schiffahrt von Ostende nach Dover

Ein großer Wunsch von mir sollte sich endlich erfüllen.
Meine Eltern versprachen, daß ich einen Freund in Lon-'
don besuchen dürfte. Ganz abgesehen von dem Wiedersehen mit ihm (ich hatte ihn seit einem Jahr nicht mehr
gesehen), freute ich mich besonders auf die Seereise. Ich

---

[1] Ich fühle mich wie neugeboren, I feel like a giant refreshed.

hatte immer schon so viel von der Schönheit der See gehört und gelesen, daß ich mich danach sehnte, diese Schönheit mit meinen eignen Augen bewundern zu dürfen. Ich wurde nicht enttäuscht. Der Reisemorgen brach endlich an. Der Wettergott schien mir sehr freundlich zu sein, und die Sonne strahlte hell vom tiefblauen Himmel herab.

Nach einer langen Bahnfahrt von Wiesbaden kam ich um 4 Uhr in Ostende an. Ich mietete mir einen Gepäckträger, um meine Koffer auf das Schiff zu bringen. Mit allen anderen Reisenden passierte ich eine Sperre, wo mein Reisepaß sorgfältig geprüft wurde. Man fragte mich, ob ich keine zollpflichtigen Sachen hätte. Ich verneinte. Nachdem ich meine Koffer geöffnet hatte, wurde ich vorbeigelassen. Ich ging über den Holzsteg auf das große Schiff. Es war ein belgisches Schiff. Ein paar Matrosen mit gebräuntem Gesicht und wetterharten Zügen liefen auf dem Deck herum. Ich sah mich ein wenig auf dem Schiff um. Ich wurde bald mit einem jungen Engländer bekannt, der diese Reise schon ein paarmal gemacht hatte und ein bißchen vertrauter mit allem war. Er zeigte mir, wo wir bequem sitzen könnten und vor dem Wind gut geschützt wären. Ein lautes, ohrenbetäubendes Sirenengeheul zeigte an, daß wir zum Abfahren fertig waren. Wir fuhren aus dem Hafen in die offene See.

Die bunten Segel der Fischerboote sahen im Sonnenschein sehr schön aus. Die See, von einem angenehm frischen Wind ganz leicht gekräuselt, machte einen malerischen Eindruck. Ostende mit seinem schönen Strand und den großen Hotels rückte immer ferner.

Wir fuhren an den Bojen vorbei, die im Wasser läuteten und sich schaukelten. Nach drei Stunden Fahrt konnten wir die weiße Küste von England sehen. Eine Stunde später plauderten die Reisenden lustig miteinander und suchten ihre Koffer, um sich zum Aussteigen fertig zu machen. Das Schiff fuhr in den Hafen von Dover ein.

Die Sonne sank schon langsam im Westen. In Dover
prüften die Einwanderungsbeamten unsere Reisepässe,
und die Zollbeamten untersuchten unsere Koffer. Ich
stieg in ein Abteil des wartenden D-Zuges nach London
und machte es mir bequem. Ich ließ mir eine Tasse
englischen Tee bringen. Dann fühlte ich mich wie
neugeboren. Gott sei Dank! Ich war seefest gewesen!

Exercise 74

He is washing himself in the bathroom. She has
already washed her hands. Have you any money on
you? Did you repair the tyre yourself? The door
opened and a tall man came in. She is dressing, I
believe. I feel very queer (komisch). Two boys were
leaning against the door, conversing with one another.
She turned quickly round. The Town Hall was in (the)
Frederick Street (Friedrichstraße). Not a leaf stirred.
He sat down on the chair. Have you shaved? They
quickly undressed. I am going to have a look round (in)
the town. You are mistaken if you think (= believe)
that I am a Frenchman. I have caught a cold. We
have proposed to visit a few friends in Bonn. We lost
our way in the wood. Do you remember the name (der
Name, des Namens) of our hotel? I am glad you have
arrived. The child lay down on the bed and wept. Why
(warum) are you getting so excited? My sisters are
having a look at the shop windows. Wash yourself!
Wash your hands! Do not turn round! Sit down,
please! I have arranged to spend a few days in Cologne.

LESSON XXX

IMPERSONAL VERBS

We must now deal with a number of Impersonal Verbs, *i.e.* those with es, *it*, as their subject.

The translation of *There is, There are*

(i) *There is, there are* (*was, were*) are rendered by es ist, es sind (war, waren) or by es gibt, es gab (no plural form). Es ist is used where the space is limited to a certain spot, es gibt when *there is* or *there are* refers to a wide or vague area. Compare the following:

> Es sind einige Kühe auf der Wiese. There are some cows in the field.
> Es gibt viele schöne Dörfer in diesem Lande. There are many beautiful villages in this country.
> Es ist kein Zucker übrig im Speiseschrank. There is no more sugar in the cupboard.
> Es gibt keine Gespenster. There are no ghosts.

Notice that es ist (sind) is followed by the Nominative, whereas es gibt takes the Accusative:

> Es war ein König. There was a king.
> Es gibt keinen Menschen, der unsterblich ist. There is no man who is immortal.

Notice further that *there was* (once upon a time) is always es war:

> Es waren einmal drei Prinzen. There were once three princes.

In inversion the es with sein is omitted, but not with geben:

> Einmal war ein Mann. Once there was a man.
> Plötzlich gab es einen lauten Krach. Suddenly there was a loud crash.

Es gibt may be used in other tenses:

> Es hat gegeben, there has (have) been.
> Es hatte gegeben, there had been.
> Es wird geben, there will be.
> Es würde geben, there would be.

There is (*are, was, were*) requires very careful thought in translating it into German. It is used so loosely and extensively in English that very often it is better to use another verb, like *stand, lie, hang, to take place, to find oneself* (sich befinden), etc. Note the following:

> Es standen zwei Männer an der Straßenecke. There were two men (standing) at the street-corner.
> Es lagen einige Bücher auf dem Tisch. There were a few books on the table.
> Es hingen einige Bilder an der Wand. There were some pictures on the wall.
> Es klopft jemand. There is somebody knocking.
> Es riefen und sangen Männer und Frauen auf der Straße. There were men and women shouting and singing in the street.
> Ein großes Fest fand in diesem Saale statt. There was a great feast in this hall.

The following verbs are always Impersonal:

> es schneit, it snows
> es regnet, it rains
> es blitzt, it is lightning
> es ist windig, it is windy
> es ist Nacht, it is night

The following are only accidentally used impersonally:

> es wird dunkel, it is getting dark
> es klopft, there is a knock
> es zieht, there is a draught
> es wird erzählt, daß . . ., it is said that . . .
> es wurde getanzt, there was dancing
> es wurde getrunken und gesungen, there was drinking and singing
> es wurde gepfiffen, a whistle went (was blown)

The following govern the Accusative:

> es geht mich an, it concerns me[1]
> mich friert, I am freezing

---

[1] Note: *That is no concern of yours*, Das geht Sie nichts an.

es freut mich, I am glad
es wundert mich, I wonder
es ärgert (verdrießt) mich, it annoys me
es langweilt mich, it bores me

The following govern the Dative:

es kommt mir vor, it seems (appears) to me
es scheint mir, it seems (appears) to me
mir ist kalt, I am cold
mir ist bange, I am afraid
es tut mir leid, I am sorry
es geht mir gut, I am well, am getting on well
mir ist . . ., I feel . . .
mir ist nicht wohl, I do not feel well
es geschieht mir, it happens to me, I happen to
es gelingt mir, I manage to, succeed in
es fällt mir ein, it occurs to me
es nützt mir nichts, it is of no use to me
es gefällt mir, it pleases me, I like

The following are Impersonal as in English:

es folgt, it follows
es genügt, it suffices
es scheint, it appears
es schlägt, it is striking (*clock*)

Exercise 75

It seemed very funny to me.　I am glad that you have arrived.　It was snowing when we left Bonn.　There were several soldiers in the inn.　Were there any ships in the harbour?　It was striking two o'clock as we drove past the Town Hall.　I am sorry, we have no more English newspapers.　Do you like it in Berlin?　She does not like her new car.　How are you getting on? Are there any stamps (die Briefmarke, *singular*) in the drawer?　Did she manage to pass her examination?[1] How many people (die Person, *sing.*) are there in the compartment?　There are no slaves (der Sklave) in this country.　It bores me to stay here.　So it appeared to me.　I have succeeded[2] in learning this difficult language

---

[1] *I pass an examination*, ich bestehe eine Prüfung.
[2] Gelingen is conjugated with sein.

(die Sprache).   Please shut[1] the window, I am cold.   He is sorry he cannot come this evening.   I felt as though I had not washed for (seit) weeks.   Is there a draught?

A NOTE ON OVERGROWN ADJECTIVES

There is one construction, of which the Germans are very fond, that causes a good deal of difficulty in actual translation.   It consists of using a long clause, including a Past Participle, as an adjective before a noun.   The clause is preceded by an article or a demonstrative, and the Past Participle is declined as an adjective.   No exercises on this construction are given in this book, as it is a difficult one to use in turning English into German; but as the construction frequently occurs in German you had better study carefully the following examples.

We might say in English, *an old man richly dressed*. In German this would run, *an old richly-dressed man* = ein alter, reich gekleideter Mann.

So the sentence, *I saw the wood that he sold to the steamers stopping there*, becomes ich sah das Holz, das er an die dort anlegenden Dampfer verkaufte.

> Die beiden, unmittelbar zusammenliegenden und nur durch eine schmale Veranda getrennten Blockhütten bestanden auch nur je aus einem Zimmer.   The two immediately-lying-together-and-only-by-a-small-veranda-separated log-huts consisted (were made up) indeed only of a single room (each).

Here all the words joined together by hyphens really make up one overgrown adjective qualifying Blockhütten.

> Jetzt hob sich langsam ihr dunkles, in Tränen schwimmendes Auge zu dem seinen.   Now her dark, in-tears-swimming eye rose slowly to his.

In plain English this might be, *she slowly raised her dark eyes full of tears to his*.

[1] *To shut* is more usually zu-machen, and *to open*, auf-machen.

Ich rette Dich von der Dir verhaßten Verbindung.   I rescue thee from the to-thee-hateful engagement.

In ordinary English we would use a verb to complete the sense: *the engagement which is hateful to thee.*

Sometimes this qualifying clause runs to great length and includes subordinate clauses within itself:

> Der alte Hermann, ein tüchtiger Arbeiter, gab sich mit dem kleinen, aber trefflich rentierenden Geschäft vollauf zufrieden, und war mit den, allen alten ihm teuren Mustern und Formen völlig widersprechenden Zeichnungen des Malers Holaus, welche ihm eines Tages sein Sohn brachte, durchaus nicht einverstanden.

> Old Hermann, a capital workman, was quite content with the little-but-exceedingly-profitable business, and was not at all in sympathy with the (to-all-the-old,-to-him-dear-patterns-and-fashions-completely-opposed) drawings of the painter Holaus, which his son brought to him one day.

In the above, all between the parentheses is really one adjective qualifying *drawings*, though widersprechenden is the only word that "agrees with" Zeichnungen.   In English we might split up this enormous adjective like this: *the drawings which were completely opposed to all the old patterns and fashions which were dear to him.*

When in translation you come across a passage that seems to make nonsense, you will very often find that one of these sentence-adjectives is the cause.   By seeing how much of the sentence you can hyphen together as an adjective you will in most cases bring out the true meaning.

PART II

KEY TO EXERCISES

Exercise 1

The brother is poor. The father is not angry. Is the uncle here? No, he is there. Is the shop not here? Yes, it is here. The baker is often dishonest. The pupil is sometimes wicked. Is the apple not good? No, it is bad. Is the garden beautiful? Yes, it is beautiful. Is the teacher always friendly? No, he is sometimes angry. Is the uncle poor? No, he is very rich.

Exercise 2

Die Brüder sind arm. Die Väter sind nicht böse. Sind die Onkel hier? Nein, sie sind dort. Sind die Läden nicht hier? Ja, sie sind hier. Die Bäcker sind oft unehrlich. Die Schüler sind manchmal böse. Sind die Äpfel nicht gut? Nein, sie sind schlecht. Sind die Gärten schön? Ja, sie sind schön. Sind die Lehrer immer freundlich? Nein, sie sind manchmal böse. Sind die Onkel arm? Nein, sie sind sehr reich.

Exercise 3

The city is very old. Is the nut ripe? The cow is not brown. The goose is not very big. Is the night not dark? Is the sausage ready? The wall is very thin. Is the hand brown? No, it is white. Is the cow thirsty? No, it is hungry. The city is not old, it is new. Is the mouse always small? The maid is sometimes very friendly. The nut is old and sour. The night is quite black. The baker is small and fat.

Exercise 4

Die Städte sind sehr alt. Sind die Nüsse reif? Die Kühe sind nicht braun. Die Gänse sind nicht sehr groß.

Sind die Nächte nicht dunkel? Sind die Würste fertig?
Die Wände sind sehr dünn. Sind die Hände braun?
Nein, sie sind weiß. Sind die Kühe durstig? Nein, sie
sind hungrig. Die Städte sind nicht alt, sie sind neu.
Sind die Mäuse immer klein? Die Mägde sind manchmal
sehr freundlich. Die Nüsse sind alt und sauer. Die
Nächte sind ganz schwarz. Die Bäcker sind klein und
dick.

Exercise 5

The song is not very beautiful. The wheel is round.
Is the village not small and very old? The egg is not
round. The roof is red. The book is not too heavy.
Is the glass not empty? No, it is almost too full. Is
the word easy? No, it is very long and difficult. Is
the child big? No, it is very small. The house is fairly
tall. Is the field round or square? It is square. The
dress is quite new but it is not very beautiful. The leaf
is long and green. Is the house not too low?

Exercise 6

Die Lieder sind nicht sehr schön. Die Räder sind
rund. Sind die Dörfer nicht klein und sehr alt? Die
Eier sind nicht rund. Die Dächer sind rot. Die Bücher
sind nicht zu schwer. Sind die Gläser nicht leer? Nein,
sie sind fast zu voll. Sind die Wörter leicht? Nein, sie
sind sehr lang und schwer. Sind die Kinder groß?
Nein, sie sind sehr klein. Die Häuser sind ziemlich hoch.
Sind die Felder rund oder viereckig? Sie sind viereckig.
Die Kleider sind ganz neu, aber sie sind nicht sehr schön.
Die Blätter sind lang und grün. Sind die Häuser nicht
zu niedrig?

Revision Exercise

Sind die Gärten lang und schön? Sie sind schön,
aber sie sind nicht sehr lang. Ist der Schneider immer
ehrlich? Ja, er ist immer ehrlich. Ist das Glas immer

voll? Nein, es ist oft leer. Sind die Städte alt oder neu?
Sie sind alt. Die Felder sind fast immer grün. Sind die
Nüsse nicht reif? Die Äpfel sind zu grün und sauer.
Ist das Haus groß oder klein? Es ist sehr groß. Sind
die Läden immer leer? Nein, sie sind selten leer.
Sind die Schüler groß und dünn? Nein, sie sind klein
und dick. Sind die Kinder immer gut? Nein, sie sind
manchmal sehr böse. Die Nacht ist lang und sehr dunkel. Der Bruder ist arm, aber ehrlich, und der Vater ist
reich, aber unehrlich. Die Lieder sind zu lang und zu
schwer. Hier ist das Dorf und dort (or da) ist das Haus.
Das Kind ist fast immer hungrig.

Exercise 7

Wir besuchen. Ihr sucht. Sie sagen. Telefonieren
sie? Die Brüder lachen. Die Väter rauchen. Spielen
die Schüler? Ihr sagt. Wir hören. Sie hassen. Sie
suchen.

Exercise 8

Träume ich? Du antwortest. Er zeichnet. Der
Onkel reist. Das Kind atmet. Hören Sie? Sie ar-
beitet. Der Bruder haßt. Ich lächle. Antwortet der
Lehrer?

Exercise 9

(a) Ich höre die Kuh. Der Onkel öffnet das Buch.
Die Mägde kochen die Würste. Wir lachen nicht. Du
suchst die Nüsse. Die Schneider machen die Kleider.
Der Bruder besucht das Dorf. Ich reiche die Gläser.
Die Kinder hassen das Lied. Sie zeichnet das Haus.
Ich lächle, aber sie weint.

(b) Wir suchen die Kühe. Ich höre die Mäuse.
Schicken Sie die Bücher? Raucht sie? Tanzen Sie
nicht? Arbeitet der Vater? Spielen die Kinder?
Kocht die Magd die Eier? Träume ich? Weinst du?
Atmet das Kind?

Exercise 10

Do you visit (are you visiting) the uncle? I look (am looking) for the eggs. The brother visits (is visiting) the shop. The tailor passes (is passing) the dress. The teacher looks (is looking) for the pupil. We hear the schoolboys (pupils). The butcher sends (is sending) the sausages. The child picks (is picking) the apple. It (he) picks (is picking) apples.

Exercise 11

Hören Sie das Lied? Ich besuche den Fleischer. Wir suchen den Lehrer. Der Schüler sucht Eier. Ich zeichne das Haus. Der Lehrer sagt das Wort. Der Vater besucht den Onkel. Sie antwortet nicht. Besucht der Onkel die Stadt? Du besuchst den Bäcker.

Exercise 12

The uncle passes the nuts to the father. The maid sends the apples to the brother. The father answers the tailor. The baker sends nuts and apples to the teacher. You pass the apple to the father. We send books and clothes to the maid. I pass the egg to the child.

Exercise 13

Der Lehrer schickt dem Vater das Buch. Der Vater reicht dem Onkel die Nüsse. Die Schüler reichen dem Lehrer die Bücher. Wir schicken der Magd Eier und Äpfel. Der Schüler antwortet dem Vater. Die Magd reicht dem Schneider das Kleid. Ich reiche dem Bäcker das Glas. Sie antworten dem Lehrer.

Exercise 14

The baker's shop is beautiful and new. The uncle's cows are big and brown. The wheels of the carriage (or cart) are round. The maid's dress is red. The walls of the house are white. The houses of the villages are small. The child's glass is empty. The teacher opens the pupils' books. The tailor's brother shows the village butcher the goose. Do you not hear the children's songs? I telephone the baker's father. The tailor's brother sends apples and nuts to the baker's child. The cow's horns are not very long. The maid's hands are small and white, but the brothers' hands are very big and red.

Exercise 15

Die Hörner der Kühe sind nicht zu lang. Ich telefoniere mit dem Bruder der Magd. Das Dach des Hauses ist viereckig und rot. Der Vater des Schülers antwortet dem Lehrer. Der Onkel schickt dem Bruder des Schneiders Eier und Äpfel. Besucht er nicht den Schneider des Dorfes? Hören Sie nicht das Lied des Vogels? Die Läden der Bäcker sind ganz voll. Der Bruder des Bäckers hört die Lieder der Kinder. Ich schicke dem Schneider das Kleid der Magd nicht.

Exercise 16

We are Frenchmen. Where do the brothers of the sailor live? They do not live here. Did you tell the sailors' song to the boy? Are the Frenchman's nephews upstairs? No, they are downstairs. Are the boy's brothers living (alive)? No, they are dead. The boys drew the lions. Did you not learn the sailor's song? We did not often visit the Frenchman's nephew. The horns of the ox are very long. They sent apples, nuts and eggs to the sailors.

Exercise 17

Wo wohnen Sie? Lebt der Hase noch? Nein, er ist tot. Schickten Sie dem Neffen des Bäckers das Buch des Jungen (des Knaben)? Wo ist das Haus des Matrosen? Es ist dort. Wo sind die Ochsen des Franzosen? Sie sind nicht hier. Ist das Haus der Franzosen nicht weiß? Nein, es ist rot; dort ist das Dach des Hauses.

Lernt der Neffe des Matrosen das Lied nicht? Rauchte der Neffe des Franzosen? Nein, er rauchte nicht, er arbeitete. Spielen die Kinder des Matrosen? Ich lachte, aber sie weinte. Wohnten Sie oben oder unten?

Exercise 18

Wir sind arm, aber Sie sind reich. Marie ist oben, und Peter spielt unten. Gretchen und Paula haben den Hasen. Er ist groß und braun. Hat der Matrose den Ochsen? Bist du noch dort? Ja, ich bin hier. Haben die Matrosen Gläser? Ja, sie haben Gläser, aber sie sind leer. Wo sind wir? Wir sind oben. Wo spielen die Neffen des Matrosen? Sie sind dort. Hast du Kühe und Ochsen? Nein, sie sind tot.

Exercise 19

The nuts and apples were not ripe. The teacher's nephew was upstairs. The maid's brothers were dead. The uncle's cows were big and brown. I had the hare, but it is dead. Was the pupil's father very angry? No, he was fairly friendly. Was the sailor's glass empty? No, it was quite full. Had you the garden? Yes, it was very beautiful. Where were you? I was upstairs.

Exercise 20

Wo war der Matrose? Er war nicht hier. Waren die Lehrer dort? Ja, und (auch) die Schüler. War der Lehrer immer freundlich? Nein, er war oft sehr böse. Hatten Sie das Haus dort? Ja, wir hatten das Haus und den Garten. Waren die Würste fertig? Nein, aber wir hatten Äpfel und Nüsse. Ich war sehr durstig, und das Glas war ganz leer.

Exercise 21

Which child is playing in the garden? This child is playing in the garden with the tailor's nephew. Were there ten cows in that field? No, there were eight oxen there. Each schoolboy had four books. In which class are you? I am in this class. Were you very poor after the war? The baker sent the nephew out of the room. In which village did you live? We lived in this village in that house there.

Exercise 22

Hatte jedes Kind fünf oder sechs Äpfel? Welcher Lehrer schickte dem Vater dieses Buch? Die drei Kinder waren in der Kirche. Ich schickte die Kinder zu der (or zur) Schule. Waren acht oder neun Häuser in dem Dorf(e)? Es waren sieben. Es sind fünf Lehrer in dieser Schule, und es sind zehn Kinder in jeder Klasse. In welchem Haus(e) wohnen Sie? Welches Lied lernten Sie? Welchen Jungen schickten Sie aus der Klasse? Welche Kuh hörten Sie? Er schickte neun Eier mit dem Kleid(e). Jedes Kind in diesem Dorf hat drei oder vier Bücher. In welchem Zimmer ist der Neffe des Matrosen? Er ist oben im (in dem) Zimmer des Onkels.

Exercise 23

der Mantel	1	des Mantels	die Mäntel
das Fenster	1	des Fensters	die Fenster
die Tür	4	der Tür	die Türen
der Stock	2	des Stock(e)s	die Stöcke
die Socke	4	der Socke	die Socken
der Hut	2	des Hut(e)s	die Hüte
die Mütze	4	der Mütze	die Mützen
der Anzug	2	des Anzugs	die Anzüge
der Knopf	2	des Knopfes	die Knöpfe
der Strumpf	2	des Strumpfes	die Strümpfe
die Uhr	4	der Uhr	die Uhren
die Taschenuhr	(as for Uhr).		
der Handschuh	2	des Handschuhes	die Handschuhe
das Haar	2	des Haar(e)s	die Haare
das Bein	2	des Bein(e)s	die Beine
das Licht	3	des Licht(e)s	die Lichter
der Tag	2	des Tag(e)s	die Tage
der Vogel	1	des Vogels	die Vögel
die Brust	2	der Brust	die Brüste
der Kragen	1	des Kragens	die Kragen

Exercise 24

The ambassador from Berlin is now in London. I sent my brother to Geneva. There are no apples in the garden. Our house is in this street. A Spaniard from Madrid is downstairs. Have you my gloves? He is the nephew of a teacher in Cologne. Where is your watch? Here it is. Otto's suit was in this room. Is this your hat? Where is Marie? Is this not your wrist-watch? This lady's nephew is dead. I pass (hand) my uncle his hat. Our cows are in the field. Marie Smith's uncle is in Paris, and William's father is in Switzerland. Fritz's sister is in her uncle's shop.

Exercise 25

Schickte er keine Strümpfe mit den Schuhen? Ihre Kleider sind immer sehr gut. Ich schicke oft meinen Neffen in Deutschland Äpfel und Nüsse von (or aus) meinem Garten. Wir besuchen manchmal unseren Onkel in der Schweiz. Schickten Sie Ihren Neffen nach Genf oder nach Rom? Die Schuhe von Max sind schwarz, und Giselas Handschuhe sind braun. Wo ist das Haus Ihres Onkels? Es ist in London. Sind die Zimmer seines Hauses sehr groß? Er schickte keine Knöpfe mit ihren Kleidern. Haben Sie eine Pariser Zeitung? Mein Onkel hat kein Auto. Schickten Sie die Bücher meines Bruders nach London? Die Häuser unserer Stadt sind groß und schön.

Exercise 26

die Fürstin	die Blume
die Eiche	das Kindlein
der Honig	die Treppe
das Leben	der Regen
die Eselei	der Edelstein
der Teppich	die Fröhlichkeit
der Februar	das Büchlein
das Gold	die Melodie
die Übersetzung	das Eisen
die Schlacht	der Löwe
der Garten	die Sonne

(das) Griechenland
die Stunde
der Jüngling
die Reinheit
(das) Paris
die Freundschaft
der Diamant
die Schrift
die Poesie
das Rauchen
der Freitag
die Frau

der Liebling
das Väterchen
die Dummheit
(das) Helgoland
der Käfig
das Tanzen
der Monat
das Pferdchen
der Kuchen
die Union
das Blümchen

Exercise 27

Have you sent the teacher's book to the baker's nephew? I have heard the lions in the wood. Has the maid not boiled the eggs? My brother has telephoned my father. I have handed my uncle his stick. This girl has played the piano. Do you like smoking cigarettes? No, I always smoke a pipe. At Christmas we send our brother apples, nuts, books and cigarettes. Do you like listening to music on the wireless? We have lived in a house in this village. The soldiers have burnt the capital of the country. My sister has looked for the advertisement in the (news)paper. We have called our dog Mops. Which book has your sister chosen? The soldiers have killed no women and children. In the summer we have often bathed in the sea. The pupils have played with the snow in the winter. I do not like dogs.

Exercise 28

Hast du geträumt? Nein, ich habe das Haus gezeichnet. Welches Buch ist auf Ihrem Stuhl? Dieser Teppich ist sehr alt. Ich höre gern Radio. Raucht Ihr Vater gern? Ja, er hat immer Zigarren geraucht. Ich rauche oft Zigarren zu Weihnachten. Im Sommer haben wir unseren Onkel in der Schweiz besucht. Haben Sie die Zeitungen nach Genf geschickt? Der Bäcker und seine Frau haben ihr Kind Margarete genannt. Der

Schneider hat das Kleid nicht gemacht. Ottos Schwester
hat Klavier gespielt, und meine Brüder haben die Musik
im Radio gehört. Hat der Schneider das Kleid gebracht?
In welchem Laden haben Sie den Hut gekauft? Baden
Sie gern in der See? Ich höre gern den Plattenspieler.

Exercise 29

I have heard nothing (I have not heard anything).
Yesterday the sun was very warm. To whom did you
send the Christmas-tree? I have sent it to my nephew.
The clouds are big and black, they bring rain. The
weather is very cold and there is fog (mist) on the river.
When did you buy this suit? I bought it yesterday in
that shop. Was it cheap or dear? It was very cheap.
The stars are small, but the moon is big. Have you sent
the wrist-watch to your sister? Yes, I sent it to her
yesterday. Has your father sent the Christmas-tree to
the children? Yes, he sent it to them yesterday. There
are three dogs on the lawn; my nephew is playing with
them.

Exercise 30

Die Sonne war gestern nicht sehr hell. Wann haben
Sie geantwortet? Es waren sieben oder acht Matrosen
auf dem Fluß. Dieser Fluß ist sehr lang. Wir hörten
kaum das Lied der Kinder. Wen haben Sie in der
Schweiz besucht? Diese Autos sind fast zu billig. Mit
wem haben Sie gestern telefoniert? Hier ist Ihr Hut.
Wo haben Sie ihn gekauft? Ich schicke ihn meinem
Bruder. Die Kinder haben die Äpfel gesucht. Ich habe
sie ihnen gereicht. Wir haben nie(mals) Nebel in
diesem Lande. Wer hat ihm geantwortet? Haben Sie
mit ihr telefoniert? War der Wind gestern sehr stark?
Der Himmel war blau, und die Wolken waren klein und
weiß. Das Wasser in dem Teich war gestern zu kalt.
Wir haben nicht gebadet. Ich habe ihm nichts gesagt.
Sie lächelte nur. Wir hörten sie kaum.

Exercise 31

The spider was big and fat; it spun a web. The bee hummed (buzzed); it flew from flower to flower and looked for honey. What does the wasp eat? It eats sugar. The donkeys brayed (were braying), the pigs grunted (were grunting), the dogs barked (were barking) and the cats mewed (were mewing). The farm-hand rode a horse. He fed the oxen, the sheep and the cows. His dog was running with him. He barked too loudly. The farmer struck him with his whip. The farmer's wife milked the cows in the stable. There are eight or nine farm-hands on the farm. They are always working. In the autumn they plough the fields. In the spring they sow. The farmer's name was Mr. Brown. He got up and began his work. He drove in his cart to the field. What did he eat? He ate bread and drank tea with sugar. His children sang songs. He gave them apples and nuts.

Exercise 32

Der Bauer fuhr zu den Feldern. Er nahm seine Kinder mit. Sie sahen gern die Kühe, Schafe und Pferde auf den Feldern. Der Junge hieß Karl. Er ritt gern auf einem Esel. Er gab ihm Heu. Der Esel frißt gern Zucker.

Karls Hund ist in dem Garten. Er ist groß und stark. Er bricht die Blumen. Karl läuft nach ihm und schlägt ihn mit seiner Peitsche. Der Hund bellt laut. Die Sonne ist warm und hell. Die Bienen summen und fliegen von Blume zu Blume. Sie fressen gern Honig. Essen Sie gern Honig? Karl sieht die Spinne nicht. Sie ist groß und dick. Sie hat ein Gewebe gesponnen. Haben Sie gern Spinnen?

Haben Sie Ihr Arbeit schon begonnen? Ich habe meine Uhr zerbrochen. Hat Ihr Onkel seinem Neffen eine Uhr gegeben? Hast du deinen Tee getrunken?

Ja, und ich habe mein Brot und meinen Honig schon gegessen.

Exercise 33

Our bank lies between the post-office and St. Mary's Church. I telephoned my brother from a call-box. There are many skyscrapers in our city. The building of the League of Nations was in Geneva, in Switzerland. There were Bolsheviks in Russia and Fascists in Italy and Germany. The soldiers are at (before) the gate of the city. They are Italians and Spaniards.

I went into the restaurant. I had a meal (= ate) and paid (for it). I came out of the restaurant and went to the market-place. I went into the cinema. The cinema was big and beautiful, but it was not a skyscraper. In the cinema there were men, women and children. I often go to the theatre. Do you like going to the theatre? I saw a hospital near the park. Opposite the big stores was the Town-Hall. This building is magnificent. I said to a policeman: "Where is there a letter-box?" He replied: "There at the street-corner." I put a letter in the letter-box. My brother is employed at a grocer's. He sells sugar, tea, etc. Behind the Town Hall was St. Paul's Church. I went under a bridge. This bridge was very high. Over the bridge travel cars and buses. The traffic is very dangerous for pedestrians.

Exercise 34

Ich legte mein Buch auf einen Stuhl. Das Wetter war ziemlich warm. Ich lief aus dem Zimmer. Ich ging durch die Tür und auf die Straße. Es war dunkel, aber die Straße war wegen der Straßenlampen ziemlich hell. Es waren acht Autos und drei Pferde auf der Straße. Ich ging mit meinem Hund um die Stadt. Mein Hund lief zwischen die Autos. Ich ging in eine Telefonzelle und telefonierte mit meiner Schwester. Sie ist in einem Krankenhaus neben der Paulskirche angestellt. Ich wohne mit meinem Bruder gegenüber dem Rathaus. Wir gingen nach rechts und kamen zu einer Brücke. Sie war ziemlich niedrig. Wir sahen auf den Verkehr. Der Verkehr ist seit dem Krieg(e) sehr gefährlich. Mein Onkel war in dem Auto. Er fuhr zum (zu dem) Marktplatz. Er hat einen Laden dort. Er fährt oft über diese Brücke. Unser Dorf lag jenseit(s) des Flusses. Vor unserem Hause stand eine Straßenlampe. Wir gingen in ein Restaurant, um zu essen. (Wir gingen zum Essen in ein Restaurant.) Nach dem Essen ging ich nach Hause ohne meinen Hund, aber ich sah ihn zu Hause, vor der Tür.

Exercise 35

Tomorrow I shall go to the market-place. What will you do there? I shall buy two or three horses. Are they cheap or dear? They are fairly dear this year. Will you go by car? Today the weather is very cold. We shall soon have (be having) snow. What will your uncle do (be doing) next Tuesday? He will fly (go by air) to Lisbon. This afternoon we shall go to the cinema. Do you like going to the cinema? My brothers will fly to Cologne one day. This evening my sister will play the piano and Else's brother will sing songs. I shall listen to the music on the wireless. I like the wireless (I like listening to the wireless).

Yesterday I got a letter from my uncle. At Christmas he will send my father a Christmas-tree. He was in France last week. The weather was very cold there. They have been having fog and rain. I have never been to France. Have you ever been to Paris?

Exercise 36

Nächsten Freitag werde ich nach Deutschland fahren. Werden Sie mit dem Auto nach London fahren? Nein, ich werde mit der U-Bahn (Untergrundbahn) fahren. Was werden Sie in Deutschland tun? Ich werde einen

oder zwei Freunde besuchen. Werden Sie mit dem
Flugzeug fliegen? Nein, ich fliege nicht gern mit dem
Flugzeug. Waren Sie schon in Deutschland? Ja, ich
war letztes Jahr dort. Zu welchem Bahnhof werden
Sie gehen? Nach Liverpool Street. Das Wetter ist
nicht sehr warm gewesen.

Exercise 37

ein großer Baum	eines großen Baumes	große Bäume
eine kleine Blume	einer kleinen Blume	kleine Blumen
kein blinder Mann	keines blinden Mannes	keine blinden Männer
ein kleines Mädchen	eines kleinen Mädchens	kleine Mädchen
welche breite Straße	welcher breiten Straße	welche breiten Straßen
der starke Hund	des starken Hundes	die starken Hunde
die kluge Kusine	der klugen Kusine	die klugen Kusinen
der taube Vetter	des tauben Vetters	die tauben Vettern (see p. 187. 6)
die häßliche alte Frau	der häßlichen alten Frau	die häßlichen alten Frauen
kalter Wind	kalten Windes	kalte Winde
derselbe schmutzige Junge	desselben schmutzigen Jungen	dieselben schmutzigen Jungen

Exercise 38

The sad girl is always weeping. German books are not
always difficult. The fat baker's little daughter gave a
letter to the old tailor's clever nephew. A clever boy
learns quickly. The little children played on the soft
grass. They do not like playing on the hard street. The
old grandfather is blind, and his old wife is very deaf.
The pretty girl is wearing a new dress with red buttons.
Charles has a clean handkerchief in the pocket of his
brown suit. The traffic in these narrow streets is very
dangerous. Two blind men went (were going) with their
white dog across the broad (wide) street. Pretty girls
are not always silly.

Exercise 39

Kleine Jungen (Knaben) sind fast immer schmutzig.
Ich werde einen alten Freund in Genf besuchen. Blinde
Männer sind nicht immer traurig. Die engen Straßen
der alten Stadt waren sehr dunkel. Ich habe diesen
unbequemen alten Stuhl nicht gern. Meine schöne
Kusine sang französische, spanische und deutsche Lieder.
Ich höre sehr gern gute Musik im Radio. Der italie-
nische Gesandte kam gestern nach London. Maries
Kusine trug ein grünes Kleid und einen weißen Hut.
Welches deutsche Buch haben Sie gewählt?

Exercise 40

The man to whom I spoke yesterday is the Mayor of
Brussels. A great film-actress plays a part in the film
which we shall see this evening. The landlord of the
"Red Lion" Inn, in which (where) I met the chauffeur
of the film-actor Willi Fritsch yesterday, has been a
sailor. The cobbler who mended your brown shoes is at
the door. The butcher served (was serving) his cus-
tomers, amongst whom was the wife of a great author.
The basket in which she was carrying the apples and nuts
was quite new. The dentist in whose house the policeman arrested the thief pulled out (extracted) my tooth
this morning. The typist who took down this letter is
dead.

Exercise 41

1. Der Briefträger, dessen Schwester unser Kindermädchen ist, hat einen Brief gebracht. 2. Der Mann,
mit dem ich gesprochen habe, ist der Neffe eines großen
Richters. 3. Die Schublade, in der (worin) ich den Brief
sah, war fast leer. 4. Die Frau, deren Mann wir gestern
in der "Blauen Kuh" sahen, ist sehr reich. 5. Der
Kellner bediente den Jäger, der bei einem sehr reichen
Kaufmann angestellt ist. 6. Der Dieb, der die Armbanduhr einer großen Filmschauspielerin stahl, ist der

Bruder eines Polizisten. 7. Das Kino, in dem ich diesen Film sah, war groß und prachtvoll. 8. Der Arzt, der meinen Neffen geheilt hat, ist nach Ägypten gegangen. 9. Die Brüder, deren Flugzeug verunglückte, sind im Krankenhaus.

Exercise 42

Die beiden (Die zwei) Mädchen, deren Vater eine große Rolle im Film "Michael Kohlhaas" spielte, hörten Radio. Der Brief, den ich in dieser Schublade sah, war von Ihrem Bruder. Das Kindermädchen, das die Kinder spazieren geführt hat, ist aus Köln. Der Arzt, dessen Neffen ich gestern traf, heilte meine Schwester in der Schweiz. Das Haus, in dem er wohnte, hatte ein rotes Dach und eine grüne Tür. Die Stenotypistin, die diesen Brief nach Diktat schrieb, hat einen Bruder, der bei Ihrem Onkel angestellt ist. Der Mann, mit dem ich gestern sprach, ist der Wirt des "Lustigen Bauers". Das Café, in dem wir ihn trafen, ist neben dem Postamt (neben der Post). Alles, was wir sahen, war weiß. Der Briefträger hat einen Brief, der von Rußland kommt. Am Bahnhof sahen wir die Brüder, die letztes Jahr nach Amerika flogen. Der Kellner, dessen Brüder das Auto der Schauspielerin stahlen, bediente den Polizisten, der sie verhaftete. Nichts, was er tut, ist sehr gut. Das Wetter war hell und warm, was unsere Arbeit leicht machte.

Exercise 43

1. Dann wohnte ein armer Fischer in diesem Dorfe. 2. Bald trafen wir die Sekretärin des Schriftstellers am Bahnhof. 3. Dann bauten die Russen neue Schulen und Universitäten. 4. Plötzlich lief der Hund aus dem Zimmer. 5. Eines Tages kam der Schneider nach Hause.

Exercise 44

1. Er ging ins Hospital, weil er krank war. 2. Da ich nicht dort war, kam er nach Hause. 3. Ich werde den Brief schreiben, sobald (wenn) ich nach Hause komme. 4. Ich werde meinen Freund besuchen, bevor ich ins Kino gehe. 5. Er trägt keinen Mantel, obgleich es sehr kalt ist. 6. Da wir eine Erkältung hatten, gingen wir ins Bett. 7. Obgleich er sehr reich war, war er sehr traurig. 8. Das Mädchen ging ins Bett, da sie sehr müde war. 9. Wenn ich sie traf, lächelte sie immer. 10. Als ich die Schublade öffnete, sah ich die Taschenuhr.

Exercise 45

Es regnete, als der Fischer über den See ruderte. Er fing keine Fische, da die Fische nicht hungrig waren. Meine Kinder hörten die Lieder der deutschen Kinder im Radio, während ich diese Aufgabe schrieb. Sobald er nach Hause kommt, wird er mit Ihnen telefonieren. Schlossen Sie nicht die Türen (machten Sie nicht die Türen zu), bevor Sie ins Bett gingen? Wenn ich nach Berlin fahre, werde ich Ihren Onkel besuchen. Da sie nicht zu Hause waren, steckten wir den Brief in den Briefkasten. Es schneite, als wir zum Bahnhof fuhren. Er spricht Deutsch, Französisch, Englisch und Italienisch, obgleich er nie(mals) in diesen Ländern gewesen ist. Sie arbeiteten, bis es ganz dunkel war. Als das (Dienst)-mädchen an die Tür kam, bat der Mann um Brot und Tee. Wir fuhren mit dem Boot über den See, obgleich es ganz dunkel war.

Exercise 46

The thief did not answer me. Did you not meet her at the station? Who gave you this beautiful book? There are many cherries and apples in the garden. Yes, I have already seen them. I shall give some to my friend. My little sister asked me for sweets. I gave her some, but she has already eaten them. "Another glass, please," I said to the waiter, but he did not hear me. At Christmas Uncle Fritz will pay us a visit. We still have some butter in the pantry. Do you like rolls with butter and cheese? We have no more oranges. Do you drink coffee with or without cream? With cream, if you have any. Both brothers were there. Have you no other bananas? I have some more, but they are not ripe. I shall buy you an ice, if you pick me some peas and beans in the garden. Have you any more tea in the pot? Is anybody at the door? I see nobody there (I do not see anybody there). They have heard everything you told me yesterday. Everyone in the village has his long garden, in which he has potatoes, beans, peas, apples, cherries, etc. People drink a lot of coffee in Germany. I had no plate, but the waiter has brought me one.

Exercise 47

Man trinkt mehr Tee in England. Haben Sie (etwas) Kaffee im Speiseschrank? Ja, ich habe ein wenig. Wenn Sie nicht genug Bücher haben, habe ich noch eines hier. Unser Onkel gab uns einige Bonbons und Apfelsinen. Ich esse gern Apfelsinen. Der Jäger trank noch ein Glas Wein. Es sind noch einige Kartoffeln im Garten, wenn Sie nicht genug hier haben. Die spanischen Mädchen pflückten Apfelsinen und Zitronen, und sie gaben uns einige (davon = of them). Haben Sie Milch oder Sahne? Das Frühstück in der "Blauen Kuh" war ziemlich billig, aber das Mittagessen im "Roten Löwen" war sehr teuer, und man gab uns keinen Kaffee. Ich esse Käse nicht gern. Ist noch etwas Zucker in der (Zucker)dose? Der Kellner hat mir ein anderes Messer gebracht, weil dieses schmutzig ist. Zum Abendessen werden wir Kirschen und Bananen mit Sahne haben. Der Kellner wird Ihnen noch etwas Suppe bringen. Jedermann war schläfrig, aber niemand ging ins (zu) Bett. All(e) seine Freunde sind in Amerika.

Einige Schafe waren auf dem Feld. Er spricht ein (sehr) wenig Deutsch, aber kein Spanisch. Wer hat all(e) die Kirschen gegessen?

Exercise 48

The father said to the children: "Do you want to go for a run in the car this afternoon to Berlin?" "Oh, yes, rather!" cried the children. They had to wear their new clothes (suits), because they were to visit their (girl and boy) cousins in Berlin. They could not (were not able to) leave the house before three o'clock, because their mother was not ready. "Can I go to Berlin by bicycle (on my bike)?" asked young Charles. "Oh, no," answered the father. "It is much too slow by bicycle. You must come with us."

Soon they were all ready. The father can drive very well. "I must buy some more petrol," he said, "the (petrol-)tank is nearly empty." So they stopped at a petrol-station. Then they came to a crossroads. The red light was showing and they had to wait. Mr. Smith's car can climb well and they travelled rapidly on the way to Berlin. At half-past three they were in Berlin. There they saw a poor motor-cyclist who was repairing a burst tyre. On (in) the wide streets of Berlin they saw buses, trams, cars, taxis and bicycles. There the traffic is very dangerous. They went up a one-way street, so they had to go backwards. Above the city they saw a large aeroplane which was to fly to America. Many pedestrians were hurrying across the street and it was (a) good (thing) that the horn (hooter) was in order. But they could always (were always able to) go pretty (fairly) quickly and overtook (passed) many other cars. Then the car stopped and Mr. Smith beckoned to a policeman. He had to ask the way. Soon, however, they were before the (their) uncle's house.

Exercise 49

Sie können nach Berlin fahren (or gehen), wenn Sie wollen. Ich soll heute abend zum Zahnarzt gehen. Darf ich hier rauchen? Ich will meinen Hund im Park spazieren führen. Er sollte gestern nach Paris fliegen, wurde aber plötzlich krank. Wir mußten zu Fuß nach Hause gehen. Weil er kein Deutsch sprechen konnte, nahm er mich mit. Sie sollen gleich zu Bett gehen. Hier spricht man Deutsch. Soll ich (etwas) Brot kaufen? Sie sollen mit niemandem sprechen. Wir konnten wegen des Nebels das Flugzeug nicht sehen. Dürfen wir (können wir) heute abend ins Kino gehen? Wir mußten mit der Taxe fahren. Wenn das Wetter warm ist, können Sie heute nachmittag im See baden. Wir wollen Ihre Kühe und Schafe sehen. Ich kann es Ihnen nicht sagen. Da mein Bruder Sie nicht besuchen kann, schickt er Ihnen einen Brief.

Exercise 50

Bringen Sie diesen Brief auf die Post. Gehen wir um die Stadt spazieren. Ich habe nach Berlin fahren müssen. Sie hat Spanisch lernen müssen. Sie haben Ihr Buch nicht finden können. Er soll morgen London verlassen. Hast du diesen Film sehen können? Er wollte nicht antworten. Meine Schwestern mußten mit dem Flugzeug fliegen. Ich kann kein Schwedisch (sprechen). Kann sie Holländisch? (sprechen: in such expressions the infinitive sprechen is often omitted). Wir haben Ihnen nicht viele Äpfel schicken können, da der Sommer zu schlecht gewesen ist. Wir konnten wegen des Nebels nicht sehr schnell fahren. Sie können (if you can is impersonal: man kann) zum Bahnhof mit dem Autobus fahren. Wollen Sie uns ein Lied singen? Ich kann nicht singen, da ich eine böse Erkältung habe.

Exercise 51

Waiter, bring us two glasses of beer, please. Taxi, drive quickly to the station! Give me an ice, please. Let us go to the cinema. Please weigh this letter for me. Please pass me the sugar. Let us go to the theatre this evening. Open the door, please. Ask the policeman the way. Let us go to London tomorrow. Please tell me where I can find a taxi. Buy me some (a few) cigarettes. Give me a London (news)paper.

Exercise 52

The Millers wanted to go to Cologne. They looked for a fast train (an express) in the timetable. Their luggage was ready. They went by taxi to the station. Mr. Miller bought the tickets at the booking-office. They had to hurry to platform nine. The porter carried the luggage. Hilda bought some sweets and Mrs. Miller chose a few newspapers from the bookstall. As the train was late they waited for a bit in the waiting-room. Then the train came in. The porter put the luggage in the luggage-van and Mr. Miller gave him a tip. They all entered an empty compartment. Hilda and Max chose the corner-seats, as they wanted to look out of the window. Mr. Miller put his attaché-case on the rack.

The engine whistled and they then set off (then off they went). As they were in a smoking compartment Mr. Miller began to smoke. He likes (smoking) cigarettes. In Aix-la-Chapelle they had to change. At half-past twelve they went along the corridor to the dining-car. After lunch they returned to their compartment. Max had to go to the lavatory, because his hands were frightfully dirty. Mr. Miller yawned. He was tired and he began to sleep. When they arrived punctually in Cologne they alighted quickly. On the platform they saw Uncle Otto and Aunt Gisela. A porter fetched their luggage from the luggage-van. Mr. Miller gave up the tickets and they left the station. They travelled (went)

up a long, narrow street and came to the house of their
(= the) Uncle. They entered the house. They were
all tired and hungry.

Exercise 53

Geben Sie mir drei Hinfahrtskarten nach Berlin,
bitte! Lehnen Sie sich nicht zum Fenster hinaus!
Träger, tragen Sie bitte mein Gepäck zum Schnellzug
nach Köln! Chauffeur, fahren Sie schnell zum Bahnhof,
sonst werde ich den Zug nach Koblenz versäumen.
Muß ich in Aachen umsteigen? Ich verließ das Haus
um halb sieben. Alle Plätze waren besetzt. Wir fuhren
letzten Montag nach Berlin zurück. Ist ein Platz für
mich frei? Der D-Zug fährt um halb zehn ab. Tante
Marie holte sie vom Bahnhof ab. Haben Sie den
Anschluß in Kassel versäumt? Ein großer Herr trat in
das Zimmer herein und sprach mit mir. Mein Hut ist in
dem Speisewagen. Wenn Sie mit diesem Schnellzug
fahren, werden Sie einen Zuschlag bezahlen müssen.
Stellen Sie Ihren Koffer hin! Wohin fahren Sie? Wo
haben Sie Ihre Handschuhe hingelegt? Wo sind die
Fahrkarten?

Exercise 54

(a) Zweimal drei ist sechs.
Viermal fünf ist zwanzig.
Fünfmal sechs ist dreißig.

Siebenmal drei ist einund-
zwanzig.
Elfmal elf ist einhunderteinundzwanzig.
Siebenundzwanzig geteilt
durch drei ist neun.
Einundachtzig geteilt durch
neun ist neun.

Vierundvierzig geteilt durch
vier ist elf.

Fünf und drei ist acht.
Neun und sechs ist fünfzehn.
Neunzehn und siebzehn ist
sechsunddreißig.
Dreizehn und vierzehn ist siebenundzwanzig.
Dreiundvierzig und achtund-
dreißig ist einundachtzig.
Achtundneunzig weniger siebenundfünfzig ist einundvierzig.
Einhundertneununddreißig
weniger siebenundachtzig ist
zweiundfünfzig.
Eintausendsiebenhundertund-
sechzehn weniger siebenhun-
derteinundvierzig ist neun-
hundertfünfundsiebzig.

Einhunderteinundzwanzig geteilt durch elf ist elf.

Dreitausendneunhunderteinund-
zwanzig weniger eintausend-
neunhundertvierundsechzig
ist eintausendneunhundert-
siebenundfünfzig.

Zweihundertundfünfzig geteilt
durch fünfzig ist fünf.

Eintausendachthundertacht-
undachtzig weniger sieben-
hundertsiebenundsiebzig ist
eintausendeinhundertundelf.

(b) Um neun Uhr—halb sieben—zwölf Uhr—vierzig Minuten
    nach eins (zwanzig Minuten vor zwei);
,, Viertel vor drei;
,, zwanzig Minuten nach drei;
,, zehn Minuten nach zwölf;
,, Viertel vor elf;
,, zehn Minuten nach elf;
,, zehn Minuten vor vier;
,, ein Uhr (um eins);
,, halb sechs;
,, Viertel vor sechs;
,, Viertel nach sieben;
,, zwanzig Minuten nach eins;
,, Viertel nach acht.

(c) Ein Drittel; zwei Fünftel; vier Neuntel; ein halb; drei
Viertel; fünf Achtel; sechs Fünfundzwanzigstel.

erste, zweite, sechste, achte, sieb(en)te, elfte, zwölfte, acht-
zehnte, vierundzwanzigste, siebzehnte, dreißigste, neunund-
zwanzigste, hundertste, tausendste.

Exercise 55

London ist nicht so groß wie die Vereinigten Staaten.
Die Erde ist kleiner als die Sonne. Die Themse ist nicht
so lang wie der Rhein. Paris ist nicht so alt wie Rom.
Gold ist nicht so hart wie Eisen. Die Stadt ist größer
als das Dorf. Luft ist nicht so schwer wie Wasser. Der
Elefant ist stärker als der Mann. Die Katze ist falscher
als der Hund. Der Knabe ist klüger als (nicht so klug
wie, ebenso klug wie) das Mädchen. Der Schmetterling
ist nicht so schnell wie die Schwalbe. Die See ist tiefer
als der See. Der Eiffelturm ist höher als der Kölner
Dom.

Exercise 56

How much do these apples cost? Are these cherries dearer than the others? These are dearest. Marie is the nicest girl in the village. Ottilie sings beautifully, Hilda sings more beautifully, but Else sings most beautifully. Which boy is the cleverest? Otto is the cleverest, but Konrad is almost as clever. Is Belgium not as big as Holland? This girl is as pretty as her sister. The older a man gets, the less he can learn. A higher (taller) tree than this (one) is in our garden. Can you speak German? Yes? So much the better. The sooner we arrive the longer we shall have to wait. The more he drank the thirstier he became. These bicycles are the best. Otto is the tallest boy in the class. It is pleasanter here in the garden than in the house. Irmgard is more diligent than her brother. We must drive more carefully through this fog. These cherries are the sweetest. The garden looks prettier in the summer than in the winter.

Exercise 57

Je fleißiger er arbeitet, desto mehr lernt er. Das Wasser ist heute kälter als gestern. Es wird dunkler. Es wurde langsam heller. Otto ist groß, Konrad ist größer, und Wilhelm ist der größte. Marie singt süßer als ihre Schwester. Sind Sie (eben)so faul wie Ihr Bruder? Dieser Junge sieht nicht so klug aus wie sein Bruder. Je länger wir hier warten, desto dunkler wird es sein, wenn wir nach Hause zurückgehen. Ich habe sehr wenig, sie hat weniger und ihre Kusine hat am wenigsten. Dieser Hund ist der treueste. Ist das Messer schärfer als dieses? Ich werde die größten und süßesten Äpfel kaufen. Der Lehrer wird dem klügsten Jungen dieses Buch geben.

Exercise 58

These gloves are mine, the others are yours. Do you always read the same paper? My house is not so big as yours. Their (your, her) garden is longer than ours. I have read my book and my brother's. I have seen his car, but not theirs (hers). Those who come (too) late must wait here. We always eat at the same restaurant. He has always lived in the same street. He who does not work shall not eat. She has found my hat, but not his.

Exercise 59

Das sind Ihre Bücher, nicht meine. Sein Bruder ist klüger als der ihrige. Mein Messer ist schärfer als das deinige. Beide Tanten wohnen in derselben Stadt. Er liest dasselbe Buch. Die, die (Diejenigen, welche) nicht fleißig arbeiten, werden nichts lernen. Ihre Bäume sind höher als die unsrigen. Sie kauft immer dieselben Bonbons. Unsere Stadt ist größer als die Ihrige. Seine Arbeit ist besser als die seiner Schwester. Sein Haus ist nicht so klein wie das seines Onkels. Die, die (Diejenigen, welche) am besten arbeiten, können früh nach Hause gehen.

Exercise 60

Last summer we spent our summer-holidays on the North coast of Germany. We packed our trunks (cases) and set out on the 28th August for Swinemünde. The weather was magnificent during the whole month which we spent there. We stayed (lived) in a large hotel which was near the beach.

Every (each) morning we got up early. After breakfast we went down to the beach. We took (brought) our bathing-suits with us and when the weather was warm we put on our bathing-costumes and caps and swam in the sea. I cannot swim like a fish, yet I like swimming. Some little children, whose parents were sitting in deckchairs, were making sand-castles. Others played football or looked for shrimps and crabs with their nets. After bathing we lay on the warm sand and sun-bathed. Soon we became very brown, almost like Negroes. One day we saw a boy in the sea. He could not swim very well. A fisherman saved him from drowning.

Sometimes we went for an outing in a fishing-smack. That was very nice and we had a lot of fun (we enjoyed ourselves). We dived from the boat into the sea. It was very nice when the waves were big. We often climbed up the cliffs, or went for a walk along the beach.

My father had hired a beach-hut and so we could have coffee in the afternoon on the beach. My father often played golf on the beautiful golf-links. We were very sad when we had to return home.

Exercise 61

Ich will morgen früh nach Stuttgart fahren. Im Herbst müssen wir die Äpfel pflücken und die Felder pflügen. Wo ist der Korb, in den ich die Äpfel legte? Zu Weihnachten haben wir vier Tage Ferien. Wir dürfen hier nicht rauchen, denn es ist verboten. Das Kind, dessen Eltern tot sind, ist sehr klug. Ich kann diesen Brief nicht lesen, weil er so schlecht geschrieben ist. Darum müssen Sie mir den Brief zeigen, den Sie heute morgen geschrieben haben. Gestern regnete es, als ich die Straße heraufkam. Der Mann, mit dem ich gestern sprach, ist der Bürgermeister. Bevor Sie ausgehen, zeigen Sie mir die Zeitung, die Sie heute morgen gekauft haben. Er ging gestern abend aus, obgleich (obschon) er krank war. Da es so spät war, ging er gleich (sogleich, sofort) zu Bett. Während er seinen Mantel anzog, hörte er jemand an der Tür.

Exercise 62

Dieser Briefkasten wird dreimal am Tage vom Briefträger geleert. Dieser Brief wurde gestern von meiner

Stenotypistin geschrieben. Ist der Brief schon geschrieben? Ich werde meinen Freund in Bonn besuchen. Das Telegramm wurde gestern geschickt. Als wir ankamen, war die Tür schon geschlossen. Das Haus ist schon gebaut worden. Dieses Kleid wurde letztes Jahr vom Schneider gemacht.

Exercise 63

Ich bin von meinem Bruder gebeten worden, nach Berlin zu fahren. Diese Äpfel wurden gestern von den Kindern des Bäckers gepflückt. Wann werden diese Briefe geschrieben werden? Das Kind ist bestraft worden. Diese Zeitung wird jeden Tag von Tausenden von Männern und Frauen gelesen. Ist das Auto schon repariert worden? Sind Sie von jemand gesehen worden? Der Briefkasten wird jetzt vom Briefträger geleert. Dieses Kleid wird vom Schneider gemacht werden. Wann wurde dieses Buch geschrieben?

Exercise 64

I thanked him for his letter. He died of gout. He was annoyed at my answer. I asked the price of the apples. He has translated this book from the German, while he was staying with his aunt. He ordered the man to wait for the train. The girl blushed at this answer. I entrust this work to you. To whom does the house with the red roof belong? Allow me to help you. I read the letter out to my mother. Describe to me the city in which (where) you live. Do you remember the day (when) we met the man? What has become of your brother? The boy (lad) leant against the wall. Follow me, please. Do you like it here in England? I do not like the English weather. You can rely on him. When did you give this wrist-watch to your sister? The others laughed and made fun of the poor boy. The little girl was afraid of the big cow. The poor man asked me for money. We trembled with cold.

Exercise 65

Die Mädchen und Jungen (colloquially: Mädels und Jungens) tanzten vor Freude. Mein Neffe ist Seemann geworden. Ich erstaunte über seinen Brief. An wen denken Sie? Fragen Sie nach dem Preis des Mantels im Schaufenster! Reichen Sie bitte Ihrem Bruder den Zucker! Gefiel Ihnen der Film gestern abend? Ich glaube (es) ihr nicht. Haben Sie nicht nach dem Arzt geschickt? Ich fürchte, daß wir morgen schlechtes Wetter bekommen werden. Ich erlaubte den Kindern, in dem Garten zu spielen. Wir erzählten dem Polizisten die ganze Geschichte. Er bat mich um Geld, aber ich schlug es ihm ab. Ich erinnere mich nicht an das Mädchen. Er regte sich über meine Antwort auf und befahl mir, ihm das Buch zu zeigen. Er lehnte sich an die Tür und wollte mir nicht erlauben, auszugehen. Fürchten Sie sich vor Löwen? Dort ist der Mann, dem wir in dem "Roten Löwen" begegnet sind.

Exercise 66

Before going to bed he wrote a letter. After reading the paper he went out. Putting on his coat and hat he ran out of the room. Bathing is forbidden here. He sat in the garden smoking a pipe. Who is the girl wearing the green hat? We heard our cousin singing. He remained standing at (*or* by) the door. Knowing he was at home I telephoned him. On looking out of the window I saw our doctor's car go by. He saw them (*or* her) playing tennis. He smoked while shaving. The little girl came running and spoke to us. I stood up on seeing the man enter, but my sister remained sitting.

Exercise 67

Als ich den Brief auf dem Tisch sah, las ich ihn. "Sind Sie fertig?" fragte er, indem er seinen Mantel anzog. Er stand bei (*or* neben) der Tür und las eine Zeitung. Der Mann arbeitete, und seine Frau spielte

Klavier. Ich bat ihn, sich zu setzen, aber er blieb stehen. Als wir die Schublade öffneten, fanden wir einen Brief von ihm. Wer ist der Mann, der auf dem großen schwarzen Pferd reitet? Wir fanden sie weinend. Bevor er ausging, telefonierte er mit seinem Bruder. Da wir wußten, daß es spät war, beschlossen wir, unseren Onkel nicht zu besuchen. Nachdem er die Annonce in der Zeitung gesehen hatte, telefonierte er mit seiner Schwester. Der sterbende Matrose bat um Wasser. Der Mann stirbt. Als ich die Straße entlang ging, begegnete ich meinem Zahnarzt. Ich kannte diesen Arzt. Er weiß nichts.

Exercise 68

I am going swimming this afternoon with my friend. Have you promised to send him a book? My uncle taught me to play the piano. I am getting (I get) my hair cut. I have had a new house built. Where did you learn to play golf? Help me to get in (i.e. *a vehicle*). Must you go home now? We shall have some new clothes made (for us) in Paris. He decided to go by car to Cologne. I decided to have my hair cut. My father has promised to meet me at the station. Do you wish to leave (set out) tomorrow? I ordered the waiter to bring me a bottle of wine. I have had a bottle of wine brought (for me). We saw him riding in the wood. Wash his hands! Have you washed your hands? I have washed his hands. The barber has cut the man's hair. Please do not cut my hair too short. Have you painted your finger-nails and plucked your eyebrows? I have my shoes cleaned. Has he gone home? They have not yet arrived. My brother flew to Amsterdam yesterday.

Exercise 69

Ich hörte Sie im Garten singen. Wer hat Sie Klavier spielen gelehrt? Soll ich Ihnen einige Zigaretten kaufen, wenn ich in der Stadt bin? Wir sind zum Bahnhof geeilt, um Sie abzuholen. Sind Sie nach Rußland gereist? Die Bäume in Ihrem Garten sind sehr hoch gewachsen. Ich ließ gestern das Gras des Rasens schneiden. Ich werde nächste Woche einen neuen Anzug machen lassen. Wir sind oft über diese Felder gewandert (or gezogen). Sind Sie den ganzen Tag zu Hause geblieben? Können Sie mir dieses Rad reparieren lassen? Ich habe Ihnen ein Glas Wein bringen lassen. Soll ich Ihnen diese Sachen zuschicken lassen? Ich habe beschlossen, mir die Haare ondulieren zu lassen. Wollen Sie mich tauchen lehren? Wir versprachen, ihnen jede Woche einen Brief zu schicken. Er bat sie, ihm zu schreiben. Haben Sie dem Kellner befohlen, noch etwas Brot zu bringen? Nein, ich habe einige Zigaretten bestellt. Wollen Sie Radio hören?

Exercise 70

Taxi, drive to an up-to-date but cheap hotel. I want to spend a few weeks in this town. Here is a good hotel, Sir, the "Riesenfürstenhof". Good! I'll get out here. How much do I owe you? Three marks fifty? (Gives him a tip.) Thank you, Sir! That's all right (Not at all, Don't mention it)! Can I have (or get) a room for a few nights? Yes, certainly! What sort of one? I do not want to spend too much.

The man said he had a few nice rooms which were quite quiet and well lighted. I replied that I should like to see them. He said I could go up by lift: Number 15. I asked where the lift was. He replied that it was in the corner. I asked the lift-boy if (or whether) the hotel had central heating. "Yes, of course!" he answered. He asked to what room I was going. I said I should spend a few days there. I asked if (or whether) the hotel had a garage. Whether the hotel had electric light (= was lighted by electricity) in all rooms. He replied that there was a bathroom near my room and that there was central heating in all rooms.

I rang for the porter. I asked him if (or whether) he would wake me up at 5 o'clock. He replied that he would not forget. I pulled up the blind and looked down upon the street.

Exercise 71

Der Chauffeur sagt, daß er fertig sei (or wäre) (or: sagte, er sei (wäre) fertig). Ich fragte ihn, ob er wüßte, wo das Hotel Bismarck sei (or wäre). Er sagte, daß er es nie(mals) gesehen hätte. Ich fragte den Polizisten, ob die Post (das Postamt) in dieser Straße wäre (or sei). Sie sagte, daß er Montag käme (or kommen würde). Das Mädchen sagte, daß sie sein Auto in der Garage gesehen hätte. Der Mann sagte mir, daß sie nach England mit dem Flugzeug geflogen wäre (or sei). Ich antwortete, daß ich den Zug versäumt hätte. Sie fragte mich, ob ich mit ihnen spielen möchte. Hoch lebe unser Freund aus Deutschland!

Exercise 72

Wenn Sie das Geld hätten, möchten Sie nach den Vereinigten Staaten (fahren)? Wenn ich Sie wäre, würde ich gleich nach Hause gehen. Wäre mein Freund zu Hause gewesen, dann hätte ich bei ihm übernachtet (hätte ich die Nacht bei ihm verbracht). Sie hätte den Zug versäumt (Sie würde den Zug versäumt haben), wenn sie nicht mit der Taxe zum Bahnhof gefahren wäre. Ich hätte mit Ihnen telefoniert (Ich würde mit Ihnen telefoniert haben), wenn ich nicht hätte kommen können. Ich sagte ihnen, daß ich ihnen helfen würde, wenn ich könnte. Ich wäre sehr gern mit Ihnen ins Theater gegangen (Ich würde sehr gern mit Ihnen ins Theater gegangen sein), aber ich war furchtbar beschäftigt. Wenn der Aufzug (Fahrstuhl, Lift) in Ordnung gewesen wäre, so (or dann) wäre ich nicht die Treppe hinuntergefallen (so würde ich nicht die Treppe hinuntergefallen sein). Ich fragte ihn, wieviel ich ihm schuldig wäre (*or* sei). Er fragte mich, ob ich dort ausstiege (aussteige). Ich fragte ihn, ob er das Licht anknipsen könnte. Er fragte mich, ob ich mit dem Fahrstuhl hinauffahren wollte (*or* wolle). Ich sagte ihm, daß ich jede Woche einen Brief von ihr bekäme (bekomme). Der Chauffeur fragte mich, nach was für einem Hotel ich gehen möchte (*or* wollte). Ich sagte ihm, daß ich die Treppe heraufgekommen wäre (*or* sei). Der Liftboy sagte, daß er einen Wecker auf den Kamin in meinem Zimmer (*or* meines Zimmers) gestellt hätte (*or* habe). Das Mädchen sah aus, als ob sie (*or* es) mehrere Wochen an der See verbracht hätte.

Exercise 73

A Sea-Voyage from Ostend to Dover

A great desire of mine[1] was at last to be fulfilled. My parents promised that I might visit a friend in London. Quite apart from the reunion with him (meeting him, seeing him again) (I had not seen him for a year), I was especially looking forward to the sea-voyage. I had always heard and read so much about the beauty of the sea that I longed (thereafter) to be allowed to admire this beauty with my own eyes. I was not disappointed. The day of my departure dawned at last. The clerk of the weather seemed to me to be very friendly, and the sun beamed (*or* shone) quite brightly from the dark-blue sky.

After a long railway journey from Wiesbaden I arrived at 4 o'clock in Ostend. I hired a porter to take my cases on to the ship. Together with all the other passengers I passed a barrier, where my passport was carefully examined. They asked me if I had any (= had not any) dutiable goods. I replied in the negative. After I had opened my cases I was allowed (to go) through (*or* by). I went across the wooden gangway on to the big boat.

[1] Ein Freund von mir, a friend *of mine*.

It was a Belgian boat. A few sailors with bronzed faces and weather-beaten features were hurrying about on the deck. I had a look round the ship. I soon became acquainted with a young Englishman who had already made this journey several times and was a bit more conversant with everything. He showed me where we could sit comfortably and be protected from the wind. A loud, deafening blast of the siren indicated that we were ready to leave. We went (sailed, steamed) out of the harbour into the open sea.

The coloured sails of the fishing-smacks looked very beautiful in the sunshine. The sea, slightly ruffled by a pleasing fresh wind, gave a picturesque impression. Ostend, with its beautiful beach and the big hotels, retreated further and further away.

We went past the buoys which tinkled and tossed about in the water. After three hours' journey we could see the white coast of England. An hour later the travellers conversed merrily with one another and looked for their cases, in order to get ready for going ashore. The boat entered Dover harbour. The sun was already slowly sinking in the west. In Dover the immigration officers examined our passports and the customs officers examined our cases. I entered a compartment of the through-train for London which stood waiting and made myself comfortable. I had a cup of English tea brought to me. Then I felt like a giant refreshed. Thank Heaven! I had not been seasick!

Exercise 74

Er wäscht sich im Badezimmer. Sie hat sich die Hände schon gewaschen. Haben Sie (etwas) Geld bei sich? Haben Sie den Reifen selbst repariert (ausgebessert)? Die Tür öffnete sich, und ein großer Herr trat herein. Sie zieht sich an, glaube ich. Ich fühle mich sehr komisch. Zwei Jungen waren an die Tür gelehnt und plauderten miteinander. Sie wandte sich (drehte

sich) schnell um. Das Rathaus war in der Friedrichstraße. Klein Blatt regte sich. Er setzte sich auf den
Stuhl. Haben Sie sich rasiert? Sie zogen sich schnell
aus. Ich will mich in der Stadt umsehen. Sie irren
sich, wenn Sie glauben, daß ich ein Franzose bin. Ich
habe mich erkältet. Wir haben uns vorgenommen,
einige Freunde in Bonn zu besuchen. Wir verirrten uns
in dem Walde. Erinnern Sie sich des Namens von unserem Hotel (unseres Hotels would sound unpleasant
after des Namens). Ich freue mich, daß Sie angekommen sind. Das Kind legte sich auf das Bett und weinte.
Warum regen Sie sich so auf? Meine Schwestern sehen
sich die Schaufenster an. Waschen Sie sich! Waschen
Sie sich die Hände! Drehen Sie sich nicht um! Setzen
Sie sich bitte! Ich habe mir vorgenommen, einige Tage
in Köln zu verbringen.

Exercise 75

Es kam mir sehr komisch vor. Es freut mich, daß
Sie angekommen sind. Es schneite, als wir Bonn verließen. Es waren mehrere Soldaten in dem Wirtshaus.
Waren (lagen) einige Schiffe in dem Hafen? Es schlug
zwei Uhr, als wir am Rathaus vorbeifuhren. Ich be-
daure (= I regret; or es tut mir leid), wir haben keine
englischen Zeitungen übrig.[1] Gefällt es Ihnen in Berlin?
Ihr neues Auto gefällt ihr nicht. Wie geht es Ihnen?
Sind einige Briefmarken in der Schublade? Gelang es
ihr (Ist es ihr gelungen), ihre Prüfung zu bestehen? Wie-
viele Personen sind (befinden sich) in dem Abteil? Es
gibt keine Sklaven in diesem Lande. Es langweilt mich,
hier zu bleiben. So kam es mir vor. Es ist mir gelungen, diese schwere Sprache zu lernen. Bitte, machen Sie
das Fenster zu, mir ist kalt. Es tut ihm leid, daß er
heute abend nicht kommen kann. Mir war, als ob ich
mich seit Wochen nicht gewaschen hätte. Zieht es?

[1] Übrig, left over, remaining; mehr would mean here no
longer, never any more.

CONCLUSION

The student who has conscientiously worked out the exercises and has followed our advice in reading German is now in a position to advance on his own account. He should buy a good dictionary; a good choice would be *The E.U.P. Concise German Dictionary*.

To obtain greater mastery of the language it is necessary to write and read as much as possible. The student who follows our advice and finds a correspondent in Germany will find he is making good progress if his German friend is conscientiously helping him with his grammar and construction. This service, to be permanent and beneficial, must, of course, be mutual. The student should endeavour to study and sympathize with the views and likes and dislikes of his correspondent. If an exchange of visits can result from such a correspondence, so much the better.

If the student resides in London he will find it quite easy to purchase German magazines and newspapers, while German short stories are becoming increasingly more accessible to the English student for a modest outlay. For this purpose let him send for catalogues of German readers to such publishers as G. Bell and Sons, 6 Portugal Street, W.C.2; Geo. G. Harrap and Co., 182 High Holborn, W.C.1; Oxford University Press, 37 Dover Street, W.1; Cambridge University Press, 200 Euston Road, N.W.1; and the University of London Press, 10 Warwick Lane, E.C.4. The student should choose at first the short easy readers, which do not cost much. These are modern stories, dealing for the most part with adventure, crime-detection and the like.

When half a dozen or so of the foregoing have been read the student can begin the study of some of the classics, such as Lessing, Schiller, Goethe, Hebbel, Grillparzer, Heinrich von Kleist, Freytag, Sudermann or

Hauptmann in drama, or Theodor Storm, Grillparzer, Jean Paul Richter, Keller, Meyer, Heyse, Freytag, Eichendorff, Hauff or von Kleist in prose fiction. The student can find details of works by the above in the catalogues already referred to. If he is interested in poetry the best anthology to buy is the *Oxford Book of German Verse*, from the Oxford University Press.

An excellent and very cheap edition of the works of the German classics is that by Ph. Reclam, Jun., of Leipzig. These can be had, either new or second-hand, from Foyle's of Charing Cross Road, and for a small sum of money the student can acquire quite a number of the best works in the literature of Germany.

The important thing is to read as much as possible, looking up just those words and idioms necessary for an appreciation of the matter. A close attention to the meaning of every word is only going to kill the interest and bring discouragement or boredom. The vocabulary and "feeling for the language" (das Sprachgefühl) will then come unconsciously and pleasantly.

By the time the student has progressed thus far upon the road, he will be able to dispense with his guide and proceed alone on a wonderful voyage of discovery, delighting in every fresh vista that opens up before his eyes. And in this interesting, nay, exciting enterprise we wish him "Glückliche Reise!"

APPENDIX A

TABLE OF GERMAN DECLENSIONS

A bracketed *Umlaut* means that not all the nouns indicated take the *Umlaut* in the plural. This is best learnt by saying for the four declensions: "Sometimes—sometimes—always—never."

1.

	Sing.	Plural
Nom.	——	(..) ——
Acc.	——	(..) ——
Gen.	——s	(..) ——
Dat.	——	——n

1. Masc. and neuter nouns in -el, -en, -er: for those taking the *Umlaut* see List 1 overleaf.

2. Neuter nouns in -chen and -lein.

3. Two feminines:
   die Mutter (..)
   die Tochter (..)

2.

	Sing.	Plural
Nom.	——	(..) ——e
Acc.	——	(..) ——e
Gen.	——(e)s	(..) ——e
Dat.	——(e)	(..) ——en

1. Most masc. monosyllables, *some not* taking the *Umlaut* (see List 2 overleaf).

2. About 30 feminine monos., *all* taking the *Umlaut* (see List 3 overleaf).

3. Some neut. monos., *none* taking the *Umlaut*.

4. Nouns in -ich, -ig, -ling, -nis, -sal.

5. A few masc. and neut. nouns with 4th Decl. plural (see List 6 overleaf).

3.

	Sing.	Plural
Nom.	——	·· ——er
Acc.	——	·· ——er
Gen.	——(e)s	·· ——er
Dat.	——(e)	·· ——ern

1. The neuter monos. in List 4.
2. A few masc. monos. (List 5).
3. Nouns in -tum.
4. Der Vormund.

4.

	Sing.	Plural
Nom.	——	——(e)n
Acc.	——(e)n	——(e)n
Gen.	——(e)n	——(e)n
Dat.	——(e)n	——(e)n

1. *All* other feminines.

2. All masc. nouns in -e (exc. der Käse, in Decl. 2).

3. Foreign words, stressed on last syllable, as der Stu-dent'.

Notes

1. Feminine nouns take *no ending* in the singular.
2. As a rule monosyllables take the -es of the Gen. sing. in Declensions 2 and 3, and words of more than one syllable take -s.
3. Words ending in -s in Declension 2 and in -in in Declension 4 double the final consonant before the ending: Autobus—Autobusse; Königin—Königinnen.
4. Notice all Declensions have -n in the Dative plural.

SPECIAL LISTS OF NOUNS

1. Nouns of Declension 1 taking the *Umlaut* in the plural:

Masculine:

Acker, field
Apfel, apple
Boden, ground
Bruder, brother
Faden, thread
Garten, garden
Graben, ditch

Hafen, harbour
Hammer, hammer
Kasten, box
Laden, shop
Mangel, lack
Mantel, coat
Nagel, nail

Ofen, stove, oven
Sattel, saddle
Schnabel, beak
Schwager, brother-in-law
Vater, father
Vogel, bird

Neuter: das Kloster, monastery

2. Masculine nouns of Declension 2 *not* taking the *Umlaut* in the plural:

Aal, eel
Apparat, apparatus
Arm, arm
Docht, wick
Dom, dome, cathedral
Fasan, pheasant
Grad, degree
Huf, hoof

Hund, dog
Lachs, salmon
Lauch, leek
Monat, month
Mond, moon
Omnibus, omnibus
[1]Park, park
Pfad, path
Puls, pulse

Punkt, point
Salat, salad
Salm, salmon
Schal, scarf
Schuh, shoe
Star, starling
Stoff, stuff
Tag, day
Thron, throne

3. Feminine monosyllables of Declension 2 (*all* taking *Umlaut* where possible):

Axt, axe
[2]Bank, bench
Braut, bride
Brust, breast
Faust, fist
Frucht, fruit
Gans, goose

Hand, hand
Haut, skin
Kraft, power
Kuh, cow
Macht, might
Magd, maid

Maus, mouse
Nacht, night
Nuß, nut
Stadt, city
Wand, wall
Wurst, sausage

---

[1] Note: plural of der Park is now more usually die Parks.
[2] Note: plural of die Bank (= *bank*) is die Banken.

4. Neuter nouns of Declension 3:

Amt, office	Gesicht, face	Land, country
Bad, bath	Gespenst, ghost	Licht, light
Bild, picture	Glas, glass	Lied, song
Blatt, leaf	Glied, member	Loch, hole
Buch, book	Grab, grave	Nest, nest
Dach, roof	Gras, grass	Rad, wheel
Denkmal, memorial	Haus, house	Schloß, castle
Dorf, village	Horn, horn	Schwert, sword
Ei, egg	Huhn, chicken	Tal, valley
Fach, subject	Kalb, çalf	Tuch, cloth
Faß, barrel	Kind, child	Volk, people
Feld, field	Kleid, dress	[1]Weib, woman
Geschlecht, sex	Lamm, lamb	Wort, word

5. Masculine monosyllables of Declension 3:

Geist, spirit, ghost	Mann, man	Wald, wood
Gott, god	Rand, edge	Wurm, worm
Leib, body		

6. Nouns, 2nd Declension in sing., 4th Declension in plural:

Masculine:

Bauer, farmer	See, lake	Strahl, ray
Mast, mast	Staat, state	Vetter, cousin
Nachbar, neighbour		

Neuter:

Auge, eye	Hemd, shirt	Insekt, insect
Bett, bed	Herz (-ens, -en),	Interesse, interest
Ende, end	heart	Ohr, ear

---

[1] Note: the plural (Weiber) is very offensive nowadays.

APPENDIX B

ALPHABETICAL LIST OF STRONG AND IRREGULAR VERBS

N.B.—(a) Verbs with a prefix having the same forms as the simple verbs are omitted.   (b) Verbs with a prefix are given when the verb is not used alone.   (c) The 2nd and 3rd singular present indicative and the singular of the imperative are given only when these forms are different from the regular forms of the verb.   (d) Verbs marked with an asterisk (*) are conjugated with sein, the others with haben.   (e) Parts of the verb in thick type indicate an irregularity in their formation.

Present Infinitive	Present Indicative (2nd and 3rd pers. sing.)	Imper. (2nd pers. sing.)	Imperfect Indicative	Imperfect Subjunct.	Past Participle
backen, to bake	bäckst bäckt	—	buk	büke	gebacken
befehlen, to command	befiehlst befiehlt	befiehl	befahl	**beföhle**	befohlen
beginnen, to begin	— —	—	begann	**begönne**	begonnen
beißen, to bite	— —	—	biß	bisse	gebissen
bergen, to hide	birgst birgt	birg	barg	bürge	geborgen
betrügen, to deceive	— —	—	betrog	betröge	betrogen
biegen, to bend	— —	—	bog	böge	gebogen
bieten, to offer	— —	—	bot	böte	geboten
binden, to bind	— —	—	band	bände	gebunden
bitten, to ask	— —	—	bat	bäte	gebeten
blasen, to blow	bläst bläst	—	blies	bliese	geblasen
*bleiben, to remain	— —	—	blieb	bliebe	geblieben
braten, to roast	brätst brät	—	briet	briete	gebraten
brechen, to break	brichst bricht	brich	brach	bräche	gebrochen
brennen, to burn	— —	—	**brannte**	**brennte**	gebrannt
bringen, to bring	— —	—	brachte	brächte	gebracht
denken, to think	— —	—	dachte	dächte	gedacht

Infinitive	du (pres.)	er (pres.)	Imperative	Preterite	Past Subj.	Past Part.
*dringen, to crowd, press forward	—	—	—	drang	dränge	gedrungen
empfangen, to receive	empfängst	empfängt	—	empfing	empfinge	empfangen
empfehlen, to recommend	empfiehlst	empfiehlt	empfiehl	empfahl	**empföhle**	empfohlen
essen, to eat	ißt	ißt	iß	aß	äße	gegessen
*fahren, to go, drive	fährst	fährt	—	fuhr	führe	gefahren
*fallen, to fall	fällst	fällt	—	fiel	fiele	gefallen
fangen, to catch	fängst	fängt	—	fing	finge	gefangen
finden, to find	—	—	—	fand	fände	gefunden
fliegen, to fly	—	—	—	flog	flöge	geflogen
fliehen, to flee	—	—	—	floh	flöhe	geflohen
fließen, to flow	—	—	—	floß	flösse	geflossen
fressen, to eat, devour	frißt	frißt	friß	fraß	fräße	gefressen
frieren, to freeze	—	—	—	fror	fröre	gefroren
geben, to give	gibst	gibt	gib	gab	gäbe	gegeben
*gehen, to go	—	—	—	ging	ginge	gegangen
*gelingen, to succeed	—	—	—	gelang	gelänge	gelungen
*genesen, to get better	—	—	—	genas	genäse	genesen
genießen, to enjoy	—	—	—	genoß	genösse	genossen
*geschehen, to happen	—	geschieht	—	geschah	geschähe	geschehen
gewinnen, to win	—	—	—	gewann	gewänne	gewonnen
gießen, to pour	—	—	—	goß	gösse	gegossen
gleichen, to resemble	—	—	—	glich	gliche	geglichen
gleiten, to slip, glide	—	—	—	glitt	glitte	geglitten
graben, to dig	gräbst	gräbt	—	grub	grübe	gegraben
greifen, to seize	—	—	—	griff	griffe	gegriffen
halten, to hold	hältst	hält	—	hielt	hielte	gehalten
hangen, to hang	hängst	hängt	—	hing	hinge	gehangen
hauen, to hew	—	—	—	hieb	hiebe	gehauen
heben, to lift	—	—	—	hob	höbe	gehoben
heißen, to be called	—	—	—	hieß	hieße	geheißen
helfen, to help	hilfst	hilft	hilf	half	**hülfe(ä)**	geholfen

Present Infinitive	Present Indicative (2nd and 3rd pers. sing.)		Imper. (2nd pers. sing.)	Imperfect Indicative	Imperfect Subjunct.	Past Participle
kennen, to know (a person)	—	—		kannte	**kennte**	gekannt
*kriechen, to creep	—			kroch	kröche	gekrochen
*kommen, to come	—			kam	käme	gekommen
laden, to load	lädst (ladest)	lädt (ladet)		lud (ladete)	lüde	geladen
lassen, to let	läßt	läßt		ließ	liesse	gelassen
*laufen, to run	läufst	läuft		lief	liefe	gelaufen
leiden, to suffer				litt	litte	gelitten
leihen, to lend				lieh	liehe	geliehen
lesen, to read	liest	liest	lies	las	läse	gelesen
liegen, to lie				lag	läge	gelegen
lügen, to tell a lie				log	löge	gelogen
nehmen, to take	nimmst	nimmt	nimm	nahm	nähme	genommen
nennen, to name				nannte	**nennte**	genannt
pfeifen, to whistle				pfiff	pfiffe	gepfiffen
raten, to advise	rätst	rät		riet	riete	geraten
reiben, to rub				rieb	riebe	gerieben
reißen, to tear				riß	risse	gerissen
*reiten, to ride				ritt	ritte	geritten
*rennen, to run				rannte	**rennte**	gerannt
riechen, to smell				roch	röche	gerochen
ringen, to struggle, wrestle				rang	ränge	gerungen
*rinnen, to flow				rann	ränne	geronnen
rufen, to call				rief	riefe	gerufen
scheinen, to shine				schien	schiene	geschienen
schieben, to shove				schob	schöbe	geschoben
schießen, to shoot				schoß	schösse	geschossen

Infinitive	2nd sing. pres.	3rd sing. pres.	Imperative	Imperfect	Imperfect Subj.	Past Participle
schlafen, to sleep	schläfst	schläft	—	schlief	schliefe	geschlafen
schlagen, to strike	schlägst	schlägt	—	schlug	schlüge	geschlagen
*schleichen, to creep	—	—	—	schlich	schliche	geschlichen
schließen, to shut	—	—	—	schloß	schlösse	geschlossen
schneiden, to cut	—	—	—	schnitt	schnitte	geschnitten
schreiben, to write	—	—	—	schrieb	schriebe	geschrieben
schreien, to cry out	—	—	—	schrie	schrie	geschrie(e)n
*schreiten, to step	—	—	—	schritt	schritte	geschritten
schweigen, to be silent	—	—	—	schwieg	schwiege	geschwiegen
*schwimmen, to swim	—	—	—	schwamm	**schwömme**(ä)	geschwommen
*schwinden, to vanish	—	—	—	schwand	schwände	geschwunden
schwingen, to swing	—	—	—	schwang	schwänge	geschwungen
schwören, to swear	—	—	—	schwur (schwor)	schwüre	geschworen
sehen, to see	siehst	sieht	sieh	sah	sähe	gesehen
*sein, to be	bist	ist	sei	war	wäre	gewesen
senden, to send	—	—	—	sandte	**sendete**	gesandt
singen, to sing	—	—	—	sang	sänge	gesungen
*sinken, to sink	—	—	—	sank	sänke	gesunken
sinnen, to think, ponder	—	—	—	sann	**sönne**	gesonnen
sitzen, to sit	—	—	—	saß	säße	gesessen
sprechen, to speak	sprichst	spricht	sprich	sprach	spräche	gesprochen
*springen, to spring, jump	—	—	—	sprang	spränge	gesprungen
stehen, to stand	—	—	—	stand	stände	gestanden
stehlen, to steal	stiehlst	stiehlt	stiehl	stahl	**stöhle**(ä)	gestohlen
steigen, to climb	—	—	—	stieg	stiege	gestiegen
*sterben, to die	stirbst	stirbt	stirb	starb	**stürbe**	gestorben
*stoßen, to push	stößt	stößt	—	stieß	stieße	gestoßen
streichen, to strike, spread	—	—	—	strich	striche	gestrichen
streiten, to struggle, quarrel	—	—	—	stritt	stritte	gestritten

Present Infinitive	Present Indicative (2nd and 3rd pers. sing.)		Imper. (2nd pers. sing.)	Imperfect Indicative	Imperfect Subjunct.	Past Participle
tragen, to carry, wear	trägst	trägt		trug	trüge	getragen
treffen, to hit, meet	triffst	trifft	triff	traf	träfe	getroffen
treiben, to drive	—	—		trieb	triebe	getrieben
*treten, to step	trittst	tritt	tritt	trat	träte	getreten
trinken, to drink	—	—		trank	tränke	getrunken
tun, to do	tust	tut		tat	täte	getan
verderben, to spoil	verdirbst	verdirbt	verdirb	verdarb	**verdürbe**	verdorben
vergessen, to forget	vergißt	vergißt	vergiß	vergaß	vergäße	vergessen
verlieren, to lose	—	—		verlor	verlöre	verloren
verzeihen, to pardon	—	—		verzieh	verziehe	verziehen
*wachsen, to grow	wächst	wächst		wuchs	wüchse	gewachsen
waschen, to wash	wäschst	wäscht		wusch	wüsche	gewaschen
weisen, to show	—	—		wies	wiese	gewiesen
wenden, to turn	—	—		wandte	**wendete**	gewandt
*werden, to become	wirst	wird	**werde**	wurde (ward)	würde	geworden
werfen, to throw	wirfst	wirft	wirf	warf	**würfe**	geworfen
wiegen, to weigh	—	—		wog	wöge	gewogen
wissen, to know (a fact)	weiß, weißt, weiß		wisse	wußte	wüßte	gewußt
ziehen, to draw, pull	—	—		zog	zöge	gezogen
zwingen, to force, compel	—	—		zwang	zwänge	gezwungen